LIFE 18 HOLES

Don Evans

outskirtspress
DENVER, COLORADO

The opinions expressed in this manuscript are solely the opinions of the author and do not represent the opinions or thoughts of the publisher. The author has represented and warranted full ownership and/or legal right to publish all the materials in this book.

Life In 18 Holes
All Rights Reserved.
Copyright © 2015 Don Evans
v1.0

Cover Photo © 2015 Stephen Howard. All rights reserved - used with permission.

This book may not be reproduced, transmitted, or stored in whole or in part by any means, including graphic, electronic, or mechanical without the express written consent of the publisher except in the case of brief quotations embodied in critical articles and reviews.

Outskirts Press, Inc.
http://www.outskirtspress.com

ISBN: 978-1-4787-6084-9

Outskirts Press and the "OP" logo are trademarks belonging to Outskirts Press, Inc.

PRINTED IN THE UNITED STATES OF AMERICA

Golf is an amazing game. However, LIFE is a never-ending adventure. How we PLAY and how we LIVE have dramatic similarities. Comparing the two brings real vision to our process of existence.

Don Evans

Contents

A HUNDRED YEARS FROM NOW,
    WHAT WILL REALLY MATTER?.. 1
A DOABLE PAR 5 6
SHORT PAR 4 – TIGHT FAIRWAY 13
BUNKERS GALORE.. 19
ELEVATED TEE 26
DOGLEG 5 – BIRDIE HOLE 31
BREATHTAKING 36
LONG PAR 3 – UPHILL 42
NUMBER 1 HANDICAP 48
EASY PAR 4 55
DON'T GET ANY STRAIGHTER THAN THIS 61
I CAN'T SEE THE GREEN 67
DECEPTIVE 74
MY "HOME HOLE" – EVERYBODY NEEDS ONE 80
HOLE-IN-ONE 87
GETS ME EVERY TIME 93
SIGNATURE HOLE 99
EASY PEASY 104
BRINGIN' IT TO THE CLUBHOUSE 109
WHAT MATTERS NOW? 114

INTRODUCTION

A Hundred Years From Now, What Will Really Matter?

"DO YOU SEE that?" exclaimed my wife as we backed out of the garage. "What?" I countered. There was a fly on the man door of our garage and she thought that incredible. Given. . . . It **is** December. The sun was hitting directly on the east end of our house -- its warmth was rejuvenating to say the least -- and that fly had responded with the audacity to take movement and emerge into the world again. Can you believe that? Well, sure you can. As our grandchildren would say, that was an "awesome" discovery for my wife. So what is *reality*? **Nature** will always be the controlling depository of the universe. That's just the way it is. It's a God thing. It is a beautiful thing. Aren't you glad man can't wrap his arms around that one and effectively change it?

And as I stand here getting ready to participate in one of the greatest games ever played, I cannot keep from thinking about how this miniscule game of golf can have such a dominant effect upon my innermost desire to succeed. You see, **I** may not matter nor may the game of golf matter a hundred years from now, but should this world as we know it still exist, God's natural nomenclature will still be AWESOME!

The fact of the matter, Raymond (just a little something between me and my wife), this game **does** matter to me. It's fun, it's challenging.

it's addicting, it's competitive, and really it is downright frustrating. But it only takes one incredible shot to rekindle a flammable desire to conquer (*conquer* not a good word) this splendid game. Is that not how life is? One small glimmer of hope and we are off and running **if** we simply have the initiative to do so. We can't blame others or other things for lack of desire or an impetus to succeed. You just have to suck it up and do it. There is a level playing field out there -- go walk on it!

    a. You see, we live in a world where: Nature's mechanics cannot be controlled or overridden by the whimsical nature of man. Incredible!
    b. Hard work and ingenuity still triumph deceptive maneuverability. Genuine!
    c. You can still get elected to an influential office not because of ability to lead but because of physical attraction and monetary entitlement. That stinks!
    d. You can be a rock star and know nothing about petrology (the study of rocks). Amazing!
    e. You can go to heaven because of what you are and Who you serve -- not who you are and what you manipulate. That's eternal!

A great thinker (Was it Einstein?) once proclaimed, "Doing the same thing over and over and expecting a different result is insanity." How are we dealing with this thing called *life* today? In any moment of time, so many things change that have a direct impact upon us. It is truly inconceivable. What we must be able to put our finger on at this moment is. . . what is that driving force in our lives that perpetuates the next action we take and the fundamental direction in which we proceed? Am I simply going to do the same ole stuff? There is a saying that "if you're riding a horse and it dies, get off!" Is that stuff getting me to the place I want to be? In reality, if it is, you probably want to keep doing it. If not, "THE HORSE IS DEAD!" Do you get it?

A HUNDRED YEARS FROM NOW, WHAT WILL REALLY MATTER?

In other words, it is time for a change. Now I know that change, even the very mention of it, scares people to death (not literally, of course). Is it not time to consider Einstein's theory? What goals have you set for yourself? Any of them need to change? Who are the people you are running with -- winners. . . losers?

Take a close look. You may need to change some of your surroundings. "But I don't want to back away from relationships and hurt someone's feelings." REALLY! Begin to count on fingers and toes to what extent some of those folks have contributed to advancing your lifestyle. (Did you get to toes?) If that person supports and enables you, hang tighter than a fly on a biscuit. But if that person creates a label of destruction for you, guess what? That biscuit simply is not edible!

Now the game of golf consists of 18 holes played in proportion to the score of *par*, *par* being the legitimate number of strokes it should take to complete the *round*, and *round* being 18 holes, of course. Speaking of *course*, all courses are different with some being very difficult to navigate according to *par* and others much easier. Then there is something called *handicap*. Every hole has a *handicap* rating, being the degree of difficulty that hole presents to the golfer. Then the golfer, after several cumulative rounds, establishes his own *handicap* which in all essence, gives indication of how good you are at competing with the course in this "greatest game ever played." (By the way, there is a movie by that title you might want to catch.)

Golf being a literal game and life being literal, how on earth do we make comparison of the two? Or shall we say, how does one stack up against the other? Let's see. . . .

Really, it is not fair to say that I will take a certain number of events in life (like 18 holes of golf), put a number on them, and then say this is exactly how I stack up. Too many variables! But it **is** fair to say that I need a comparison, or in all honesty, am I living up to *par*? But *par* in what? What about my spiritual life, mainly my relationship with Jesus Christ? Just going to be honest here. We need to be a "scratch" player when it comes to this relationship. *Scratch* means in golf that you are competing with the course and shooting par consistently. If you are consistently below par, you are really good and probably need to consider going on tour. PGA tour that is. So how are you and your best Friend getting along? Just for the record, this needs to be a "fly-on-a-biscuit" relationship. After all, He <u>will</u> stick closer to you than a brother. How much are you talking to Him each and every day? And even more importantly, how well are you listening to what He is having to say to you? What is your score on this one -- par, better, not-so-better? Regardless of how good it is, what can you do to cultivate an even better score? Also, how much initiative is there on your part in sharing your score with this best Friend with someone else? Might be an excellent opportunity to look up that guy who by relationship was creating a label of destruction for you. Odds are, if he affected you that way, he may be ruining someone else's life. That guy needs a moment of decision, an element of change, a direct encounter with excellence. . . and <u>you</u> may be the one with the expertise to enable them all. How 'bout it? Lots of questions, huh?

How difficult is the *course* you consistently find yourself on? *Links courses*, as they are called, usually present narrow fairways with tall grass rough to contend with. Man, that stuff is hard to get out of! Needless to say, you probably can't even find your ball. Are you experiencing any tall *rough* in your life? Sometimes, simply navigating down the narrow fairways of life is difficult enough, let alone contending with that rough stuff. At times you have probably found yourself feeling like a lost ball in high weeds.

Who has your best Friend (remember. . . that One that "sticks to you closer than a brother") put in your life to help you circumvent some of the rough spots? Don't be afraid to ask for advice. Everyone needs a mentor. If God has placed that special person in your life, take full advantage of the situation. Think with me. . . . God doesn't make junk and He created you and He won't throw junk in front of you. Hey, getting out of the *rough* is tough but not impossible -- not even improbable. Thank God for His providence and move on.

In golf there is something called a *penalty* stroke if you have to lay

A HUNDRED YEARS FROM NOW, WHAT WILL REALLY MATTER?

out of the rough. Simply put, means you lost a shot to par. You may realize that you in fact may have created your *life penalty*. Listen. Take a stroke! It is not the end of the world. Remember. . . there is another hole to play. We go through life making up strokes all the time. Just the way it is. Live with it!

What's that thing called *handicap*? What about it? Life doesn't always play out easily. *Handicap* in the dilemma of life is the degree of difficulty that is being experienced at any given point in your existence. How do you prepare for it? What is your level of education -- is more an option? What is your earning power -- do you need to increase your current skill set? "Hump level" is what you want to get over! How physically fit are you? I believe there is a direct correlation between physical fitness and mental acuteness. Sure, there will always be exceptions. But that doesn't mean you get off the hook. MAN UP! Remember. . . we don't blame something else for our own ineptness. So how will you lower your *handicap*? Lower *handicap* means a better score in this thing called *life*.

So. . . in a hundred years what will really matter? You want the truth? EVERYTHING will really matter! Why? No, you probably won't be around, but the seed you plant now will be the seed that produces tomorrow's growth. The mold that you produce now will be the mold that will be improved upon in the future. Your legacy must be futuristic. Your children's children matter. They are not going to be nobodies in a nothing world. Just like you, they must be the catalyst for a coming age. Yep! A hundred years out they will probably be asking, "What will really matter a hundred years from now?"

Hey, let me challenge you to 18 holes of life. (Oops! I almost said *golf*.) Are you up to it? Show me #1 tee box!

CHAPTER 1

A DOABLE PAR 5

IN KENTUCKY AND points north and east, playing golf is very hit-and-miss this time of year. After all. . . it is almost Christmas. But it is also a fantastic time for those of us who have been blessed with family and friends and who look forward with great anticipation to the most wonderful season of all. Unfortunately for others, like a guy I met with today, Christmas will be a very depressing experience – abandoned by family, and friends are few and far between. In my opinion, no matter who you are, everyone needs a "doable par 5" in their life.

As I stand on #1 tee visualizing the flight of life down the center of the fairway, I see bunkers guarding the right side with a steep embankment which spells out-of-bounds to my left. If I choose, I can allow my off-the-tee to be rather frightening. After all, life isn't dealing well with me because I can't even see the green. So what one thing must be imperative in my life right now? FOCUS! Where is life taking me -- or better said -- where am I taking life?

After a few practice swings (And by the way, isn't life full of practice swings?), I am finally standing over the ball and the shot that can -- if I choose to let it -- be the propelling force for the rest of my life. Surely by now you have surmised that golf is being used as an analogy for life. Now. . . FOCUS! But to focus I have to concentrate and to concentrate I have to reach down inside myself and pull out something called *determination* that I believe lies within the recesses of everyone's being **if** they have the guts to jerk it out. Is it easy? Probably not! But is this thing called life a "doable par 5?" I think so ! How badly do you want it is the question.

A number of years ago, I made one of the most exciting decisions of my life. I asked the most beautiful, talented, and remarkable specimen of female flesh God had ever created to marry me. I was totally focused on her and my concentration was laser-like. DETERMINED! Had she said "No," I would have been devastated. But she didn't and my determination was rewarded with the most fantastic three- letter word I had ever heard. "YES!" My wife has made life so vividly pristine for me. But it didn't stop there. We have been blessed with two tremendously determined and disciplined children.

Also a number of years ago, I made the decision that has changed my life for eternity. That decision carried a name with it – Jesus Christ – and He convinced me that I had been wonderfully and fearfully made and that His Father was determined to take controlling interest of my life. I surrendered and He made good on His promise. But you know what? He never promised that there would be no out-of-bounds to the left side of the fairway of life. As a matter of fact, He said there would be bunkers and plenty of 'em. He told me that sometimes the most perfectly visualized tee shot is going to find its way into the sand. Oops! Remember. . . first hole is a "doable par 5." Doesn't mean you may not make a bogey once in a while or maybe even a double. But let's get back to the tee shot.

The guy I mentioned earlier. . . let's call him Joe. Joe is looking down the same fairway I am. Think a minute. Did you ever wonder why it is called a *FAIRway*? Joe sees the same out-of-bounds and the same bunkers I see, but he looks at them differently. Growing up wasn't glamorous for him and his adult life has gone from bad to worse. Marriage went wrong, children have rejected him, he has no one, and nowhere to turn. Really? REALLY! You see, Joe was confronted with that same man I was. Remember His name? Jesus! Now granted, Joe has a different perspective than I have, and that's okay

◀ LIFE IN 18 HOLES

because Jesus has become his best friend. Joe now has hope and hope is THE most gorgeous spectacle that any of us have never seen. His visual fairway may seem awfully narrow, but remember: It is called a *FAIRway*!

Now, bunkers on the right. . . out-of-bounds to the left. All I have to do is avoid both and I can visualize a perfect tee shot right down the middle. This one is crucial, but I can see that perfect landing area. You don't believe it, do you? But my Titleist Pro V Life -- I mean Pro V1 -- landed in an exceptional spot. Little less distance, I would have been standing below the ball for my second shot.

Think with me. . . . I have always struggled when looking uphill at my goal and wondering, "Can I really pull this thing off?" A little to the left would have put me in the rough. And whether you realize it or not, yes, the rough gets its designation for a reason. Rough places in life are not always so easy to get out of, just like on the golf course. But I visualized the shot, hit it solid because I concentrated on the ball, and it landed perfectly. First shot and it looks like a "doable par 5" -- or could it possibly be a birdie?

Close your eyes for a moment and imagine the most advantageous position you have ever been in. At that particular stage of development, you could truly get a handle on where you were taking life. It was as if you had just fallen right smack in the middle of the best landing area of your *FAIRway*. What could be better? But at this point, extreme caution is absolutely essential. You see, when it looks like that second shot could not possibly fail, we have a tendency to hurry our backswing, fail to follow thru, or just flat chunk it. Disastrous results! You find yourself still 250 yards out when actually your third shot should have been an easy chip to the green, possibly facing down a birdie attempt. What am I saying? As the old saying goes, "Don't get the cart before the horse." You have an incredible lie on the perfect spot of your life's *FAIRway*. . . advantage is yours. Don't blow it! No rash decisions, no deceptive maneuvers that you may think would increase your potential, no dishonest practices. Just step up as the incredible person of character that has gotten you to

A DOABLE PAR 5

this advantageous position and hit it out of the park. Oh, no! Wrong game! Hit it straight down the middle of the *FAIRway*. Nothing in life will ever afford you more potential than honesty, integrity, dependability, and trustworthiness. Those are the essential ingredients of your **character,** and without them you are destined to **bogey** the first hole in life. Fortunately, second shot is coming up.

Second shot! Remember: Focus, concentrate, visualize the shot. MECHANICS. Doing the good things over and over precisely is essential. The mechanics of a golf swing are much like those practice swings of life talked about earlier. Remember my two tremendously determined and disciplined children I didn't really introduce you to previously? Much of that discipline and determination come from seeing parents willing to take the necessary practice swings in life. Granted, they saw that incredible specimen of female flesh they called Mama and their not-so-perfect Dad make several bogeys as we traversed this thing called *life*. But every now and then they even witnessed a few birdies. Hole-in-one? Well. . . later. Am I ever going to hit that second shot?

Perfect! Second shot lands. Extraordinary angle to a pin set far back right on a beautifully sculptured undulating green. But I'm still about sixty yards from the stick. Pull off a meticulously placed third shot and I'm home free. Somebody said. . . did you say *free*? Even though I'm sure it happens, I personally have not experienced much *free* stuff in life. I don't play the lottery and my wife's first name is not JEANNIE (as in a bottle), but I am a little bit familiar with something called WORK! My dad always taught me to work hard and incredible advantage could be had. Bible says, "If you don't work, you don't eat." Doesn't get much simpler than that. Hard work and ingenuity have always been the backbone of our American ideals. And God help us if we allow them to slip into oblivion. Those two precious commodities I call my children are voracious workers who understand the dire need for it if they are to traverse through the complexities of human life. Deep breath. . . . Everything is in place for my third shot. All I have to do is EXECUTE.

Club selection is my next obstacle – a mind thing. Do I pull a 7 iron, keep the ball low, and run it all the way to the pin? After all, I do have a level lie. Or do I use a more lofted club, drop it down close to the pin, and try to check it up with some backspin? Decision! You know, life is full of decisions. We can ponder all the pros and cons and interject every conceivable scenario. You will do well by doing so. We can pray -- and I definitely recommend bathing every major decision in prayer -- and don't forget the minor ones either. There is always a "gut" digestion to every decision. Just don't let it roll around too much.

Finally, we have to pull the trigger. Use every available resource but always bear in mind: God has directed you through countless opportunities, allowed you to traverse your way around the cautions and into the constants, and the results have been measured up as tremendous experience. Never forget to use your God-allowed experience when executing that final mental process that excites you to say, "**This is it**!" Guess what? I just pulled the 7 iron.

Again, it is a visual process. Never execute the shot until you can see in your mind the result. Hey, man, that's life. Life is visual if we will only take a close look. Where do you want to be five years from now? Can you see it? Remember the second paragraph. . . . Where are **you** taking life? Evaluate your options. Focus laser-like attention on completion of your goals. Digest every morsel of info you have at your disposal, take a deep breath, and relaxing, let half of it out and hold steady as you squeeze the trigger on that all-important decision.

Never **jerk**! The decision didn't come without considerable fortitude, so why risk missing your target now? Stop. Think. There is a ubiquitous God that has His hand on every diverse detail. Trust Him! Consider the insight of discerning people He puts in your path. Did you know that every pro golfer consults with his caddy **before** taking those crucial shots? Decision time is time for you to crawl into the driver's seat of the rest of your life, rev up that engine of extremely well-thought-out calculations, and pop the clutch on infinite travel

A DOABLE PAR 5

into the future. Have you got it in you? I just laid the 7 iron on the Pro V1 and watched it roll to a stop seven feet from the pin. Goodness! This is for birdie!

I just left it short. Now why did I do that? Have you ever asked yourself, "Why?" Sure you have. But you see, the enemy of every man's/woman's soul will travel the greatest of distances to use that *why* against you. **Why** – because you are inferior! **Why** – because you don't have the intestinal fortitude! **Why** – because you are the weak link in what otherwise would have been an unbreakable chain. The arch enemy has a decisive answer for everyone's *why*.

Get a **grip**! The worst enemy of best is second best. Never quit one effort short! And even though you may feel you are at the end of your rope, "tie a knot in it and hang on." (Joe Beck, a tough ole cowboy, said that.) And listen to what Christine Caine, author and traveling preacher said: "Satan on his best day couldn't defeat me on my worst day." **Why**? Because the Lord himself had a plan to prosper her and give her a hope and a future. (Jer. 29:11). Use the distance between you and the avenue of success to motivate every dimension of your physical and mental abilities. NOW. . . read the green. This putt is for birdie.

Can you believe it? This putt is for birdie! How much break can you see? How fast is the green? Will I push or pull this putt? All variables. But life is full of variables. What are some of yours? You say, "Too numerous to mention." Simply reduce them down to a self-controllable number. A few odds are very overcomeable. Don't stack the deck of indecision against yourself. I just struck that putt beautifully. . . .

Dagnabbit! I just missed that seven-footer for birdie! You were sure I was going to make it, weren't you? Disappointed? Sure! "**News Flash**"! I still made **par**! Remember the title of this chapter: "A Doable Par 5". Hey, I didn't fail. I just didn't excel. THIS TIME! Hey, man, this is only hole # 1 – I have 17 more to go. Could I possibly shoot a 72 today -- par golf? Well. . . .

My next challenge is a "short par 4 with a tight fairway." But

LIFE IN 18 HOLES

remember. It is a *FAIRway*! How has your challenge in life begun? Someone said, "Today is the first day of the rest of your life." Guess that means we start now. Just a reminder. . . *FAIRway*. Everyone has to play the same hole.

CHAPTER **2**

SHORT PAR 4 – TIGHT FAIRWAY

GAZING DOWN THIS very tight fairway on #2, I suddenly realize my most aggressive nature is swelling up within me. Yep, there are hazards on both sides that close in really tightly, BUT this hole is drivable. Do I pull out the big stick, risking penalty if I miss-hit it just a little bit? Or do I play more conservatively? Play safe and par is definitely doable. Take the risk and birdie can be had. Kind of like life, isn't it?

When I was young -- before wife and **definitely** before kids -- the stuff out there didn't seem to carry with it the weight that it does today. I kind of operated on the theory of "win some, lose some." Now that is not too bad because I had always heard, "Show me a man that has never failed and I will show you a man who is a failure." In other words, that man had never tried anything. That used to be easy to say and still is, but actually pulling the trigger on a big-ticket decision today seems to be more threatening. So do I hit driver and go for it? Or do I pull a fairway metal, lay up (so to speak), and probably look at an easy second shot? The big stick really moistens my ego right now, but. . . .

Life. . . . We really do find ourselves bombarded with enticing opportunities, none of which we have to bite on. Then there are those few that really arouse our competitive spirit and create an almost aggravating adrenalin rush. What to do? Think! Am I well informed or

LIFE IN 18 HOLES

is excitement of the moment overriding patience and wisdom? Now this excruciating opportunity may be a tremendous potential business venture for the entrepreneur, or at least one that plays in my future capacity to earn income. Simply put, I could be staring a really good job right in the face. Regardless, recognition and tolerance must be your supporting partners in this decision. A very well-known business exec once said, "I find it very easy to get into something but I find it extremely difficult to get out."

So let me throw something else out. What if this opportunity that is presenting itself is simply one of cultivating, strengthening, and increasing a relationship that should be crucial to you? What do you do with that one? No wonder we hear so much about relational quagmires; it seems we are doing very little to cement relationships. I am talking about deeply intentional, lasting relationships.

Just the other day my wife and I were having what she called "lunper." It wasn't lunch and it wasn't supper -- it was in between. As good a designation as any, I guess. A man and his companion (wife?) were ushered over to the table next to us. Now I wasn't being nosey, but I couldn't help but observe their actions. Drink orders were taken, server leaves, and there was no conversation between the two. Then almost immediately this guy takes out his phone and gives it all his attention while paying zero attention to his lady. She is simply looking around while he is totally engrossed in this heart-stopping apparatus called iPhone. Maybe it was a Droid. Whatever!

My wife excused herself to the restroom while I took care of the bill. And right before I left, there was acknowledgement from this guy that someone else was at his table. Amazing! Then. . . back to the phone. GIVE ME A BREAK! Don't get me wrong. Our gadgets are very useful and extremely helpful. But do they supplant personal relational experience or guarded investment in those individuals closest to us who should be arousing our most competitive interests? Seems we are always longing for something to fulfill us, but are we looking in all the wrong places? The Bible says, "A man is to love his wife as himself and that she will respect her husband." (Ephesians 5:33) A

SHORT PAR 4 – TIGHT FAIRWAY

little advice to the man at the table next to me: Concentrate on her and it may astound you as to what you will get in return.

In golf, competing against the course seems to really turn us on. Today though, standing on the tee box on #2, I really want to par this hole. Tee it low, hit it straight with the 3-wood -- that is the plan anyway. Let's see if I can pull this thing off. Focus. . . mechanics. . . . It looks really good, lands, and gets a good roll. I jump in the cart all pumped about the next shot. Then I stop to think. The golf cart really makes it easy to maneuver around the course and takes out so much of the work. I don't have to lug around that heavy bag full of clubs and other paraphernalia. Usually, driving right to the next shot is an option. This is so easy! Just like this cart, in life we tend to take so many things for granted. If we are not careful, we will allow ourselves to become content. I know contentment is great gain, however. . . .

For many a good job, nice warm surroundings, and relatively good health so often lull us into becoming complacent. Complacency and taking for granted the good stuff around us are very dangerous. Some years ago it seemed job security was a given, but not so much anymore. There will always be that aggressive pursuer who is staring you down if you fail to produce. Or perhaps the company you are working for finds itself needing to "cut back" in order to compete in the marketplace and they are asking you to sacrifice in order that all succeed. You have always assumed that great hourly wage would just be there and now you have to make a choice.

I recently spoke with a middle-aged woman, working a very menial job, who shared a very provocative story with me. The company she had worked for eighteen years was experiencing strong market competition and asked their employees to share the burden for a while, taking a pay cut. You could sense her frustration as she lamented, "It wasn't even that much per hour." As she put it, day turn workers with lots of seniority said they could not live on less. They didn't believe management would stand on their word and close the plant. Guess what? Admittedly, she had not planned ahead, therefore losing everything she had worked for all those years – house -- everything.

◄ LIFE IN 18 HOLES

She said she would get <u>some</u> compensation but not until she was 67. Long time! Speaking of planning ahead. . . .

In golf you should never "hit the shot" until you visualize or **plan** the next one. My grandsons really enjoy playing pool when they come to our home to visit. I am trying to teach them that even though it is fun to make that shot that presents itself right now, you need to playshape for the next shot. "Hey, boys, running the table is much more exhilarating than making one straight in."

In life we need to "playshape" for each and every next move. It is called *planning ahead*. Don't take anything for granted. Use your God-given mental capacity to plan your shots for the future. Visualize where you want to be five years from now, set goals, and be aggressive in reaching those goals. You may have to compromise once in a while on your most ultimate planned scenario. But failing to plan ahead will find yourself out of the loop. Put in the time necessary **now** so necessary time will be available tomorrow.

Sixty yards out -- lob wedge for my second shot -- life is great. Life <u>is</u> great! We need to gobble up every morsel as we travel through it. Never back down from the hard work and hard decisions that will propel you into the realm of financial independence. Of course this destination is different for all of us. It is kind of like the Scott Trades commercial: "I don't trade like someone else. I trade like _____." (Insert your name here.) Finances are important but never neglect due diligence when cultivating relationships with family and friends. Do for others. Remember the golden rule? Treat your wife like the queen she is. Or maybe it's just your girlfriend. Lavish her with excellence -- doesn't have to be monetary. Find her most crucial needs and take care of them. Next to spouse, treat children as your most valuable resource. Provide for them and make time with them. Think. . . they provide you with grandchildren. What a trip! One good friend is worth a thousand acquaintances. Put a number to it. How many good friends do you have? Fingers? Or perhaps fingers and toes? That many would be exceptional. Guard those relationships. They are very rare commodities these days.

SHORT PAR 4 – TIGHT FAIRWAY

Did I tell you that I really want to make par on this hole? I didn't fall for the ego trip and go for broke. My advance planning has paid off – I just stuck that lob wedge to within three feet. If I can putt a lick, I shall have exceeded my expectations and walk off this hole with birdie. Success! Don't you feel good when you succeed?

A long time ago when my son was younger, he took up a sport that I had participated in for most of my life. He became very proficient, to say the least, in the world of archery. Lots of practice, plus hour after hour of shooting in both the rain and the cold as well as the good weather, launched him into competitive arenas. Winning smothered him with trophy after trophy and soon his mom and I were carrying him all over the country to compete in tournaments. Success had its rewards and resulted in free bows and equipment from a well-known manufacturer. But let me tell you what meant more to me than all of that. When I was growing up, my dad taught me to hunt. I will never forget his patience. His natural ability to teach was extraordinary and he invested vast amounts of his time in relaying valuable insights to me. I tried to do the same for my son. I will never forget showing him how to look for deer sign, locating the best places to put his tree stand, and being patient enough to wait for the optimal time to shoot. Leaving him in a tree stand one cold morning and trusting his learned skill returned dividends. When I came back to check on him, that big grin was evidence enough of success. I am sure I remember that day much more vividly than he. That little buck was a treasure and I will never forget his **success**.

Success is contagious! Treasure every minute of it. Build your momentum on what you have accomplished and gravitate toward loftier ambitions as your successes multiply. Remember. . . . You are competing against the course. It is absolutely phenomenal!

I am not going to miss this one. Sure, it is just a fun round of golf but my heart is pounding. Whether or not I make this putt is not going to make or break anything, but your competitive nature **does** matter. Without it there is very little opportunity for success. How badly do you want it? What price are you willing to pay? What has life laid at your doorstep today that you are unwilling to fail to take advantage of? Be a fanatic when it comes to conquering the dreams stored up in the cranial atmosphere of your very being. Don't settle for! EXPRESS yourself!

There is no sweeter sound than that Pro V1 dropping to the bottom of the cup. I just made that 3-footer! As I put the flagstick back in the cup, I am reminded of just what it means to make birdie. That is one better than par! The course just said to me, "You defeated me – at least on this hole." Think what the course would say if eagle was had or perhaps even a hole-in-one. Is this not crazy fun?

Walking off # 2 to get back in the cart that will convey me down a steep hill and up the other side to # 3, I can't keep from thinking how thankful I am not to be walking this course. I am reminded: Don't take things for granted. There is so much to be thankful for -- even the small stuff. I read a book once titled *Don't Sweat the Small Stuff*. Interesting! I like this next hole.

CHAPTER **3**

BUNKERS GALORE

A *BUNKER* IS a defensive military fortification designed to protect people or valued materials from falling bombs or other attacks. Needless to say, we are not referring to a military situation wher trying to execute a particular hole in golf -- # 3 in this case -- and beat the course by dropping that little round ball into a 4.25 inch diameter hole in less than the given number of shots for par. So whose bright idea was it to call sand traps or other encumbrances on the way to the green *bunkers?* I don't know -- neither do I really care.

    This I **do** know. Strategically placed bunkers or traps can cause major disturbances for the person who would attempt to defy the duplicity of any well conceived and engineered hole-layout from tee to green. Please don't get me wrong. I am not saying that hole #3 is dishonest in any way, but it **is** downright TRICKY! When you step out of that fantastic machine called the golf cart, probably pull driver, walk to the tee box, and swallow up the beauty of what lies in front of you, you probably think this is simple enough. Come to think of it, I believe some golf course architects are a little dishonest or at the least very deceptive because they want you to think this thing is a lot easier than it is. Did I ever mention that golf is a mental game?

    Why don't we stop right here and do some mental calculation In order to succeed in this game called *life*, you must never give in to the allurement of stooping to deception in order to **get ahead**. In business or simply in dealing with the constant fluctuations – the ebb and flow of life –we need to project ourselves as "bunkers" for the benefit of others. In military terms remember, bunkers are defensive mechanisms. We need to be protectors of people and their stuff. *Stuff* being their legitimate right to interact with us and others, whether or not we would do it that exact way, as long as they are being genuine and realistic.

In business we must accept the common ground of competition and maneuver with integrity in rhythm to the parameters around us while maintaining our own viability, as long as our counterparts are being honest and forthright with us. That doesn't mean that if our competitors choose to use illegitimate tactics that we retaliate with vigor. It **does** mean however, that we constantly need to engage in the fundamentals of **fruit inspection**. I believe I read in that best seller called the BIBLE that honesty is a great virtue. Everyday life is really no different. Treat 'em good, treat 'em right, protect their stuff, and become known as a "bunker." Whatever you do, protect others from bombshells and attacks.

So you say to me, "Why is it I see so many out there using illicit tactics who seem to be thriving in this thing called *life*?" All I have to say is. . . they will get their reward! Read the "good book." It is full of those regrettable stories. Never be one of those people. If they are willing to prostitute their values for what they consider to be gain, so be it. Don't get caught up!

Number 3 green is fortified with bunkers that defend it well from the most ambitious golfer in his pursuit of defiance of this gorgeous kidney-shaped green. However, it has given up one line of defense: that being the right front which allows total accessibility and begs for attention from the average golfer. Come on, guys, sometimes we have to be realistic. Forget the green though. I'm not even off the tee yet and I'm already worried about hitting that thing! Slow down. Did I use the word *tricky* somewhere?

Fairway is fairly wide but the architect just happened to place **bunkers** down the right side. He wouldn't do that, would he? Cart path runs alongside of those babies and ridiculously thick rough just to right of the path. Might I add (for me anyway), that right side just seems to draw my Pro V1 that way and that usually is not too good. Did I say that strategically placed bunkers could result in major disturbances? Ever had any of that stuff in your life?

Listen. . . . I deal with **minor** stuff. Did you ever notice I like that word *stuff* pretty well? But **major** -- maybe that's why I had a bit of trouble with core classes in college. They were always a part of my MAJOR! Well, that was a while ago. Major problems due to disturbances seem always to be personified. Whether we like it or not, people are a part of our lives. I don't think man was really created to be a hermit, so that means we are destined to have interaction with others. Disturbances many times result, and reacting positively to those adversities can bring out our greatest personal characteristics **if** we will only allow them to. Patience and persistence are both necessary. Patience allows you to cope and deal with, while persistence permits you to fight a good fight, finish the race, and keep the faith. Paul said that to Timothy when he realized he was not much longer for this ole world. But Paul was looking back. I encourage you to keep those thoughts in **front** of you as you quell major disturbances of life and upload those dubious thoughts into the **minor** category of personal perception. Let me make a suggestion: Commit scripture to memory. The inspired Word equips and perfects! Did I tell you I really like this hole? Might I add. . . this hole is anything but simple.

Zero wind, sun coming across the back of the box -- what more could I ask? The ball seems to be traveling pretty well today, so all I have to do is concentrate, focus, and split the fairway with my tee shot. Come to think of it, that's all you have to do on **any** tee shot. Why is it always much easier said than done? Let me ask a huge question. Any of you guys out there have a daughter? Heck, yeah, you do! And when it comes to looking out for that mesmerizing little bundle of your DNA, you will protect her to the hilt. Listen, guys, you know exactly what I am talking about. That little female organism can do more to ignite reaction in you than the power of the cosmos ever could. Yours may be little now or maybe you've turned your head and she has become a beautiful young lady. Let me tell you something based on experience. She will always be your little girl. It is kind of like that "easier said than done" golf shot. God introduced daddies to their little girls so that He could shatter every conceivable element of realistic manly resistance. Talk about a string around your finger! You never want to let go. Raising girls is easier said than done! Be patient and let me share a story with you.

In the book of Genesis we are told that "a man shall leave his father and mother and be joined to his wife, and they shall become one flesh." Just so happens those intentions are the same for that little girl whom Daddy wants to never let out of his sight. She grows up and guess what? (Yep! But that doesn't mean you have to like it.) I won't burden you with wedding details, but I do need your understanding here.

Coming home after all the festivities, I began to realize how empty our house felt. I climbed the stairs and walked down the hallway to my daughter's room. It was then that the most excruciating feeling of loss reached out and grabbed me. For the first time I was no longer her counselor, no longer her provider, and no longer the only man in her life. (Hey, guys, cut me some slack here.) I sat down on her stool in front of her dresser and I could not hold back the tears. Bunches of tears. . . . I was still her father but it was necessary for her to leave. I really hadn't given up anything, but at that particular moment I thought I had lost **everything**. Life really has its moments! I am told that I am to "embrace the process" -- that the process is greater than the destination. Being honest, I haven't always put my arms around that one too well.

Standing over this tee shot is absolutely exhilarating! I have a totally relaxed feeling about this one. Excellent contact and I watch as my ball comes to a stop just beyond the 150-yard marker. And that marker, by the way, is right in the center of the fairway. That keeps you coming back. Life really cries out for those seemingly rare moments when you are so at peace with a decision or action and you just have that "gut" feeling that everything is perfect. That could be those "few and far between" occurrences that we desperately need. That, my friend, keeps you coming back.

A good, solid 8 iron pin high is what I need right now. And then, I look out at those dreaded bunkers. Why is it that all those big holes full of sand can wreak such havoc on the psyche of one's mental awareness? We simply have to deal with situations in life that are less than optimal. Giving up is not an option and bailing out just to get out is totally arbitrary. (Or should I say absolutely stupid?)

How many of you have ever read that little book in the *Bible*, "Philemon"? In the story, Paul asks Philemon to receive back into his company a slave who had run away, perhaps stolen from him. But not just to accept him – rather to receive him as a brother. It is very easy to contemplate Philemon's decision and totally miss out on the once slave, Onesimus. Paul is commending him as once useless but now useful. You know what? Onesimus, in my opinion, had options. Out of fear, he could have chosen to run after he left Paul's company. Certainly we are not told the whole story, but we can surmise the outcome. I believe he chose to go back.

Think with me. We face a lot of situations in life, that in our own strength, we are going to fail. With the help of others like a Paul or more importantly, accepting the help and friendship of Jesus Christ, we can face down an awfully lot of less than optimal situations. Just a thought. . . . Your best friend or could-be best friend Jesus, does not help a man escape his past and run away from it. He enables him to face his past and rise above it! Now what about you? Man up! Stare down those bunkers. It is time to hit a great shot into # 3. Just where I planned: wide right, a long way from the pin, tucked just behind a bunker on the left. But I am dancing on this green. In case you didn't know, that is just a term for "I'm safe on and putting."

Big break from right to left. . . about 35 feet. . . I can see this line really well. Before I make this putt, however, I want to share with you two of the goals I have set for myself this year. By the way, when you evaluate where you are going and have a mental picture,

◀ **LIFE IN 18 HOLES**

a visualization, write down that picture. Visit it often and tweak it when necessary. (I think we have talked about that.) One of several goals I have set for this year is to "break 80" consistently. Yep, talking about golf, and that is a very important goal. What that would mean? I am constantly getting better. Better at what? Focusing, visualizing, concentrating, and mechanics. Each of these is extremely pertinent in whatever we are doing in life. I need -- it is a self-evaluation thing -- to get better at whatever, and in the coming year at golf.

Listen. We <u>must</u> have the mentality of **master**: superiority . . . excellence. . . . The most splendid adjective you can attach to your desire -- mentally download that bad boy and strive to attain it. You see, my golf score may always or <u>will</u> always fluctuate some, but my efforts to get me to my goal must remain steady and constant. Hey, guys, you are no different. Issue an ultimatum to yourself, pull the trigger on the goals you need to accomplish, and let nothing deter you from your dream. Get READY! A friend of mine always says when you ask if he is ready, "Just like pork and beans." He is ready!

Another goal I want to share is not only important but it is emphatically necessary. I will take two trips (call 'em vacations if you want) with my wife this year. She is the love of my life, the symbol of points future, and I MUST embellish her. I must do the math to figure out how to pay for those trips, plan the details of those two trips, and sweep her away twice to places that will model her intrinsic value to me. You see, she is my security, my all, and my strength. God gave her to me and if I will listen, He will direct my every movement toward her. Hey, guys, guard your wealthy possession!

Good solid putt. Did I tell you I really like this hole? Man, I left it just 10 inches short and it was dead on line. Every touring pro gets more disgusted with himself for leaving a putt short than any other part of his game. Good instructors tell you to visualize the ball stopping a foot beyond the cup. In other words, give it a good run and don't leave it short. In life, in every task you set out to accomplish, put enough emphasis on each effort so as to never come up short. Set lofty goals, scale them back if need be, but when you decide to "jump the ditch," make sure you pick yourself up on the other side!

Just a tap in! Know what? I just made par. That means that I am one under through 3 and my day is getting gooder and gooder. I think I told you that I really love this hole!

CHAPTER **4**

ELEVATED TEE

NEVER HAD ONE, witnessed only two, and statisticians say the odds of an average golfer making a hole-in-one are 12,750 to 1. The two I've personally seen? A good friend of mine, whom we will call S.R., poured one of them in from this elevated tee on # 4. The other. . . my son engineered. And we will talk about that at length in chapter 14. Average golfer? Don't know if I would call my buddy an average golfer. Matter of fact, I really wonder just what I would refer to him as. Truth has it though, none of us who play together quite often are very good. When you get as old as we are, you become enthralled to realize you still have enough energy to roll out of the cart, hit the shot, and manage to climb back into that four-wheeled miracle that will usher you up to your next experience. Nah. . . not really. We are not <u>that</u> bad yet!

Number 4 is simply a gorgeous piece of human ingenuity! From the blue tees (playing those today) middle of green is usually 160ish. Looking down on this marvelous spectacle, the apron in front of the putting surface is cut really short, creating a very tight lie if you come up a little short. On either side of the front access are sand traps that are deep. Don't want to be in either of these bad boys. Putting surface is large and today the pin is far back right. We are looking at 175 from tee to pin today and the placement will challenge any pretty decent golfer.

ELEVATED TEE

What I have yet to mention, the elevation drop from tee to green is probably 40 feet. Now that doesn't sound like much -- and it isn't -- but club selection is critical. Depending on wind and weather conditions and marker placement on tee boxes, this shot could call for a wedge or 7 iron and it always seems to put me right in between clubs. These variables always play to the golfer's anxiety, cause an adrenalin rush, excite the unexcitable, and make for a downright fun shot. Can you believe that? Hey, man, this elevated tee shot rocks!

Have you ever been in a situation in which you just know you have to do what you have to do yet you expect limited results? Happens in life, you know. That's why it is <u>so</u> important as we play this game of living that we never take our eye off the potential for excellence and the possibility of stupendous outcome in what would ordinarily be "settle for" finishes. Life has not been given you by God to squander! You have been created for excellence. Take Thomas Edison for example: "He led no armies into battle, conquered no countries, and enslaved no peoples," yet through the ethos of invention and entrepreneurialism, he emancipated the lives of millions. He held 1093 patents for inventions but it took him 3000 attempts before actually conquering the invention of the light bulb. His inquisitive nature resounds and he was always working at seemingly menial tasks that resulted in shocking results. When might <u>we</u> stumble upon mind-boggling results when we actually think our actions are only superfluous? It is kind of like S.R. Remember my buddy with the hole-in-one?

Let me tell you, S.R. in his wildest dreams could not imagine what was about to happen. Did I mention odds of 12750 to 1? Rains had been torrential. . . ground was sopping wet. . . . S.R. pulls an 8 iron that should have been **way** too much club, and hits it perfectly. When I say perfectly, at least right at it. Landed short even with that way-too-much club, hit the apron in front of the green (and by all rights should have plugged in that wet stuff), took one bounce, and rolled directly into the bottom of the cup.

Are you kidding me? If I have done my math correctly, if S.R. played golf every day (which he doesn't -- not even close), and played four par threes per round, it would take him 8.56 years to beat the odds. Give me a break! But he did it. I saw it!

Forgot to mention, he is playing the white tees. My point being, if you never take that shot at life regardless of how dismal you think it is, you will never see success drop in the bottom of the cup. Don't stop one effort too short. Results may be staggering.

While I stand on this beautiful elevated tee, I can't help but marvel how blessed we are to have been created as equals and turned loose to explore the infinite threshold of the universe. The unfathomable beauty of that which we have been dropped into the middle of is liberating at the least and unquestionably angelic in scope. To lose a moment of our unquenchable thirst to progress in this atmosphere would be sheer absurdity.

Downhill with a pretty good wind blowing from our back, I believe this is reachable with 8 iron. With pin tucked back right corner and a trap to make it over, I am visualizing back center of green all the way. Good round going so far. Get this ball up high and let it ride the breeze and continue the quest for a sub-par round. You never know. . . .

Total concentration as I approach the shot and then something in the peripheral stops me cold. It is kind of like that PGA player at the start of his backswing and the "photographer's click" – probably sounds like someone just pulled the trigger on a .44 magnum to him. That is how much those guys concentrate.

This time it is something fantastically different. Stopping to inhale this distraction. . . coming out of a grass bunker to the left back of the green with destination the high grass beyond the cart path to the right, a mother skunk and two little ones waddle right into view. And let me tell you. They are in no hurry and far be it from me to dissuade their journey. I will simply wait this one out. Could say here, "THAT STINKS!" Such is life, right?

Unfortunately, way too often we let things that are destined to happen upset us and cause what could be irrretrievable pain that is unnecessary. In other words, we allow strong emotion -- call it anger or temper and you would be right on -- to take hold and blur our sensible perspective. Lashing out at those who are dear to us and whom we love the most due to some trivial response to a matter that matters not is just plain idiotic. But it seems we all do, don't we?

Or painting a business associate into a corner which leaves no other room but for him/her to retaliate has no grounds for debate. Common sense seems, in so many cases, not to be so common any more. Thinking just a little bit rather than thoughtless demonstrable action wins every time. Listen. If there is a skunk in the room, quietly open the door and let it out rather than chase it around the perimeter. You lose every time.

Finally, the wait is over, the all-clear is sounded, and it is time to line up this shot again. Focus. . . mechanics. . . . Remember? Pull this one off and life is so much better. It really matters, however, how you pull it off. Life is a game of character. Uprightness is totally admirable. How you are viewed by your peers is a direct reflection of how you carry yourself. Demand respect by being respectful. Demand loyalty by paying the price of being loyal. Let your ego be a direct reflection of your outgo. Hit life's shot with integrity and it will be dead-on every time. Back to that 8 iron to the middle back of green. Stuck it DEAD ON! Oh, to savor the results of a well- planned shot!

8 iron back in the bag. . . racing down the cart path to make this putt. Did I ever mention you have to think positive? I notice how dark the horizon is to the west. Funny, but I had paid no attention to the growing storm threat.

Often we become so engrossed in what we are doing in the immediate that we allow the near future to become obscure. I am certainly guilty of only seeing my need for existence in the present while totally obliterating the identity of others that surround me. Surely you have never done that! In other words, I become so consumed in self -- sometimes absorbed in the plight of my self-made dilemmas or just merely reticent toward those around me -- that I fail to notice the approaching storm either in my own life or the debacle rapidly maturing in an unsuspecting soul near to me. It is time to step back. View the landscape. Positive encounters with reality need positive formation in the consciousness of awareness and thoughtfulness. Let me make a suggestion. Give yourself unsuspectingly to someone whose storm is fierce in its intensity. Cradle their despondency, venerate their circumstance, exhibit great compassion, and simply stand close by when someone is desperately needed. Be a storm chaser to someone.

Hey, man, I have to hurry. It's getting darker. You know, I planned this shot and left it just where I wanted it. Why the rush? Just a storm coming! But we do have a tendency to **rush**. Usually, it will affect the outcome every time and in life, rushed decisions can be devastating. Hit the pause button! Seek advice from that storied accomplice. Stay the course and weather the storm. Listen. *Life* – just like this putt -- is just too important. Now, go through the pre-shot routine. Wind is blowing pretty good right now so allow for the ball to drift a little more to the right. Get your distance right and mentally envision this putt. Have confidence that you are ready, check your mechanics, and let's do this thing boldly.

So let me just go ahead and give you the results. I didn't make the putt but I got it close. Tap in for **par**! As much as I relish this moment and set my sights on #5, I really look forward to the remainder of this uncertainty called *life* and can't wait to see what God has in store for tomorrow. And tomorrow is enough because I am not much of a multi-tasker.

Listen to me. When I start my last EVER backswing in this incredible journey of life that my heavenly Father has afforded, all I am looking for is a good, smooth follow-through. With eternity looming, I won't be disappointed in not making birdie, eagle, or certainly not hole-in-one. It is going to be exhilarating to hear my Father say, "**Par** for the course! Well done, my good and faithful servant. You just played BOGEY FREE!"

As I put the pin back in the cup and walk off #4 green, it is just beginning to rain.

CHAPTER 5

DOGLEG 5 – BIRDIE HOLE

IT IS FLAT pouring now. What's the ole saying? "Raining cats and dogs." Pulling up to #5 tee box, I am glad the windshield is up on this cart. It is "shielding" me from the brunt of the rain as I position the cart directly into the teeth of the storm. Just have to wait this one out. This time of year the weather can change abruptly, and hopefully this one will dissipate as quickly as it appeared. I am relatively dry but just as importantly, must make sure my tools of the trade, my clubs, are protected as well. Got it. Sit it out. Ooh, this is a cold rain.

As I sit here thinking -- and by the way, that is a very dangerous thing for me to do -- life thoughts consume me. So many people fail to prepare for or shield themselves from coming storms. Never forget that preparation time is never wasted time. And I am not referring to situations that loom large with little preemptive disclosure. Hey, man, I am talking about life. Life can be so harsh, totally gruesome, brutally relentless, and devastatingly intolerable. Yet we tend to walk up to it as if the world is completely defenseless against us. Get a grip! We need to **prepare**.

Think. . . . We purchase life insurance with no intention of using it, but actually what we are doing is preparing for someone else resulting from our own demise. Time to prepare for a lightning bolt is **before** it strikes you. Life is coming. Time to activate defense mechanisms is **before** the enemy attacks. Make sure your windshield is up in order to shield you from all those darts that are being hurled at you. Prior to your "tools of the trade" being tarnished by unanticipated and unmitigated disaster, shield them from what simply will come sooner or later and make restitution before it happens. Life can be so sweet when we pick her fruit **before** the storm destroys it.

Rain over. "Oh, what a relief it is!" With this front passing through, the air is much cooler; time to layer up. Toboggan takes over for the cap, pullover fleece greatly adds warmth to my upper body, and a pair (that means two) of winter golf gloves really bring a lot of comfort. Did I mention **preparation**?

You know, sometimes it is the really meager things that bring so much pleasure to life. Stop to think. Doing incremental things that are not obnoxious to others and certainly soothing to you is just simply neat. And think again. You don't even have to have others' approval for doing them. So once in a while, allow yourself to be extravagant in a menial way and MAN UP to this thing called life.

Speaking of things that bring pleasure, my son and daughter-in-law have a dog. It is a Labradoodle. (Did I spell that correctly?) Well. . . whatever! His name is Titus and to say the least, that guy is a hoot! For him, food is an obsession. Could I say a romantic intoxicant -- visions of sugar plums dance in his head. Titus automatically gravitates to whomever has a morsel of anything with a delectable offering to it. Hilarious, he will lay his head on your leg and look longingly at you with anticipatory eyes. Usually, you can't resist and give in to his remedial advances. The remedy of course for him is something luscious to gobble up, and I believe everything to him is luscious. Furthermore, he has a way of growing on you. My daughter-in-law has always been infatuated with him. He is her baby! My son, on the other hand, seemingly wanted to remain aloof. . . seemingly. We were visiting them the other day and he finally fessed up. "I would do anything for that little guy," he said. Could I say, "Titus rules the roost!" God knew we all need a little pleasure in this thing called *life*, so He inserted the dog as a little quirk of providence. Man's (woman's) best friend. Unequivocally, a true statement.

DOGLEG 5 – BIRDIE HOLE

Tee it up, man! Got to do something to get the adrenalin and the warmth motivated. This long dogleg right par 5 is one of my favorite holes on the golf course. Don't ask me why, but making birdie quite often may have something to do with it. Doing things right and reaping right results have a way of maximizing a man's inexorable demeanor. In other words, it gets you pumped and *pumped* is a maneuver we all enjoy. Charging ahead under control is exciting and man! I just launched that tee shot! Best drive of the day leaves me in the middle of the fairway, past the dogleg, and I will be able to see the green. Still a long way out, but I can put vision to my goal, the green and the pin -- a combination that may just render a birdie. This is exhilarating, but "Come on, man!" If we let it, life dishes out a lot of these experiences. We just have to be **prepared** to take hold with earnest.

In the cart. . . . This four-wheeler can't even run fast enough to get me to my next life adventure. Standing over a perfect lie with 3 wood in hand, I am <u>not</u> going to miss this opportunity. Have you ever noticed? In some things and usually under the same circumstances, you usually seem to perform well. Could we attribute that to confidence? Let me insert something here. Confidence is unassuming! It comes pretty natural when we are prepared to perform. When we are confident, we are not afraid to take a stand – not necessarily because we know we are always right, but we are not afraid to be wrong. Life needs confident expression!

Confident, controlled, smooth swing. . . and I just landed my Pro V1 ninety yards from the pin. A perfect distance for my sand wedge is all that's left. Speaking of a confident life, don't ever let one defeat or possibly being proven wrong on an issue bring destruction to an otherwise phenomenal life experience. Own your mistakes, subordinate your insecurities, and plunge headlong into a prolific existence.

I can taste the opportunity for birdie. Ever been that way? Don't it feel good? You just sense that the process will end in impeccable results. Hey, man! It simply does not get better than that. Let me interject. The saving grace introduced by an almighty God to totally undeserving man is the epitome of not getting any better!

We have a tendency to talk about a lot of perplexities in this life, but I personally believe more people struggle with the enormity of death than any other issue. The gravity of it looms with serious perception. However, if we have accepted Jesus Christ as our personal Savior -- and bar none, everyone is given opportunity -- believe it or not, death is only the consummation of having been given literally the epic adventure of wielding our way through LIFE. It is with skill and ease that we can master the road course of life **IF** in fact we yield this personage of ours to Jesus and anticipate death as the exuberant vehicle it is to extrapolate the bliss of future immortality that *man's eye has not seen, nor has man's ear heard, nor has it even entered into the heart of man what God has sculptured and mobilized for us in heaven*. When we anticipate death with the anticipation of what it truly affords, we can then accept life even in total obscurity because of what follows this precious journey through time.

Concentration preempts this next shot. This green is really tricky if I leave my ball above the hole. It is fast, break is brutally hard to see, and confidence (there's that word again) will be seriously diminished if I leave it long. Life requires concentration. Never neglect the minute particles that make up the intricacies of life decisions regardless of how minuscule they appear to be. I want this shot to have a lot of loft, carry about eighty yards, and check up with a minimal amount of roll -- and did I say leave it below the hole? Wa-lah! Perfect execution! I envisioned the shot and pulled it off. Hey, man, take a really close look at the shot you have in life and pull it off. Do not allow circumstances to hinder your success in executing your on-ramp to an exciting future, both in this life and for eternity.

Composure. What in the world is that? By definition, "the state or feeling of being calm and in control of oneself." In case you haven't been keeping up with the number of shots from tee on this par 5, THIS IS FOR BIRDIE! I think I told you I usually play this hole pretty well and right now, for this putt, my confidence is at its pinnacle. Absolutely no break. What do they say? Straight as a stick! (I wonder

DOGLEG 5 – BIRDIE HOLE

what imbecile came up with that.)

Crunch time! You make the call – did I make it? You know it! Had to make that one. This is a birdie hole, remember?

I only wish I had the vernacular, plain ole ordinary language, to explain the awesome sense of accomplishment I enjoy right now walking off this green. It is seismic -- tremendously unexplainable! The beauty of creation that surrounds this setting simply adds to the euphoria of this moment. As I think about the atmosphere in which I now find myself, anticipate the breathtaking beauty of the next hole, and relish the sheer splendor of life, I ask myself: Why are so many people searching through artificial means and commodities hoping to enlist in something real that has meaning?

Hey, man, for the benefit of someone else and their future and not with any thought of gain or pride for self, take someone by the hand and pull them out of the utter exhaustion that they are experiencing in life. Explain to them the necessity for an accomplished life and lead to that type of destiny by example. There is a world full of people out there who desperately need you to make a *birdie* for their sake. Be a difference maker. It takes **confidence**.

It just occurred to me – this next hole is truly BREATHTAKING! You have got to be kidding me! You won't believe it. . . just started spitting snow. Well, after all, it is December. Things change pretty rapidly around here this time of year. This too shall pass.

CHAPTER **6**

BREATHTAKING

IF ONLY YOU could be here with me at this precise moment. Some would say this is our drabbest time of the year -- that they can hardly wait for spring (they must). But oh, how picturesque! BREATHTAKING! The topography is second to none. This course was carved out of a 450-acre farm and the natural lay of the land was left relatively unchanged. Should I say, unblemished! I would have to admit that in spring and in the fall it is supercalifragilisticexpialidocious! Spring. . . everything is gorgeously green and the cool breezes seem always to be blowing across this particular tee box, number 6. The fall brings a myriad of colors that are almost indescribable and enormously beautiful. Hence, the title of this chapter. To my left, actually bordering # 16 fairway, I can see the namesake of the course, an old rock silo that history would have to undo its years. Still as solidly formed as ever, probably never to be used again, the trademark of Old Silo Golf Course looms serendipitously above the landscape. Her silhouette, an epic timepiece, has generated untold conversations that find themselves slithering through clubhouses all over the country.

Sometimes I wonder if I really pay enough attention to things around me. All of this was created, I was placed in the mix, and if for no other reason, it was brought into existence just for me to enjoy. I cherish the solitude of the moment in which I find myself. Not deserving nor due to any service rendered on my part, the gratuity of this experience is overwhelming.

Elevated tee that finds as its destiny a brilliantly shaped green on a similar elevation as the tee box, this par 4 is anything but easy. Dropping way down to a semi-level fairway guarded to the left by three huge bunkers and a creek that meanders squarely through the middle of this fairway, tee shot needs to stay a bit left allowing for a good approach to this elevated green. Too much to the right and you find yourself in rough, usually cut six inches or more. In addition, a right lie into this green means crossing two large and deep sand traps that seem to obliterate your view of the green. Other than that, nothing too much to be concerned about EXCEPT a huge sycamore tree looming large just beyond that creek I told you about. Can't even imagine how long this thing has been around. Its long limbs stretch out over the fairway and they inevitably seem to find a way to interfere with an otherwise reasonably decent shot. Much to my chagrin, not only is there a tree, a creek, tall rough, and bunkers to contend with, but also the elevated green has several undulations and drops miserably from top to bottom making for tremendously fast putting. You know though, this is a beautiful hole.

Getting back to that sycamore. . . . The name derives from the Greek language meaning fig-mulberry. The sycamore of the *Bible*, a species of fig, was native to the Middle East and eastern Africa. The American sycamore, which grows so vigorously around here, seems to have very little intrinsic value -- doesn't even make good firewood.

So we ask, "Why even a part of creation?" Good question! But just as good, the question: "Why do I exist?" You see, the sycamore lends no credence to how we determine its value. It is just there. You and I though, we can choose to simply exist and live out our allotted days OR we can choose to contribute meaningfully to society and bring relevance to our own reference. Our choice. I personally believe that you were conceived (and <u>you</u> must perceive) and put on this earth to make a difference. It is no one's obligation but our own to quantify and qualify how we will do that. Unlike the sycamore, however, we must take authority for our conception, acquaint ourselves with the rules of engagement, and move to modify the direction of society so as to make a difference. That is a challenge. Get after it. Start turning the rocks of your life over and see what fascinating adventures lie beneath. Rhetoric is not sufficient; results alone will illuminate the landscape.

Pulling driver, as I stand on the blue tees, my goal is the 150-yard marker, middle of the fairway. Concentrate on a smooth swing and complete follow-through. I need solid contact. Let's do this thing!

Pro V lands with little roll and farther right than I had wanted. Not too bad -- not in the rough -- and fortunately, the pin placement is left and back on as level a piece of turf as I could possibly wish for. Back in the cart, I begin my descent, navigating the switchbacks on the cart path. This baby is steep and speed is not an ally. Several carts have had to be pulled out of the holler as a result of overly aggressive Formula One type drivers. Not a good thing! Anyway. . . made it to the bottom and now find myself looking uphill to the green for my next shot.

In life, have you ever found yourself not in the rough but yet not in an ideal position in the fairway? In these kinds of situations, you really don't know whether to lay up or **go for it**. Sometimes practicality is a virtue, while at other times an aggressive nature seems to steal the spotlight. Of course <u>you</u> have to make that call, but I have found that timid reaction does not necessarily align itself with sought-after aspirations.

What are you looking for? Is it advancement in your current job? Maybe a career change? Or perhaps something totally bizarre or even personally intimidating? Ponder this. . . . Next guy out there looking may be of the very aggressive nature. Who wins? You or the next guy? Again, <u>you</u> are the one who has to pull the trigger. Be adept to your options, but never shy away from the potential for being prolific.

Hey, man, there is no way I am laying up! Even though I am standing a bit above the ball, a good solid 7 iron and I will be putting for birdie. I like the possibles. Come on! I need to make this shot. Good contact, really good distance, so it was the right club. But I pushed it.

BREATHTAKING

This will be a long putt severely downhill and super fast. Ah, what the heck! It may not look nearly as intimidating when I get up there as it does from here. What about some optimism?

Crossing the fairway to the cart path, I think about the future and my confidence toward it. Successful outcome? What will my legacy be? The spin-off of my life and how it impacts others and especially how it contributes to the legitimacy of my children and grandchildren. . . . Will it be credible? Hey, man, we cannot afford to live our lives with tunnel vision. Our character, integrity, honesty, and value will have -- should have -- an eternal impact on others. Our lives must be a one-man conspiracy, not by definition in a harmful way, but our aim must be to enhance and inspire the lives of the ones we desperately love and admire. God has created us with so much solubility. How we will allow our very nature to dissolve into and give formality to our sons, daughters, and grandchildren is of enormous consequence. With finite time remaining -- of course that is true of everyone but especially of us older boys -- crucial is the context in which we must live our years. Oswald Chambers made the statement, "Leave the irreparable past in His (God's) hands, and step out into the irresistible future with Him." You may have noticed I am very good at issuing decrees. (I would rather refer to them as challenges.) But listen, my friend, the way to take charge of your future and change the future of others is to walk alongside the very nature of THE IRRESISTIBLE GOD! If you haven't already, allow God to extrapolate your very being. Then conform to His specific direction for your life, and improvise as He gives you hope to affect the lives of others with magnitude. That is called *living life to the fullest*. EMBRACE IT!

Well, back to what is at hand. As I begin the climb up the hill to # 6 green, I consider how cold my body would be without that extra clothing that was stored in my bag for my consumption. There is no way I am taking my gloves off to attempt this putt. At times it is almost hilariously exciting to realize that you did actually plan ahead and had the mental sobriety to eliminate to some extent a degree of physical anguish. Isn't it funny how times like these make you think of long-gone days that you could have actually done without?

Thirty-six years ago -- hardly seems possible -- Kerry (my wife) and I had just brought the most wonderful little bundle of female flesh home from the hospital. Just turned 1978 and with the new year came the new snow. Day after day, highways and streets were closed with only single lanes being grudgingly kept open to allow travel for necessary and emergency vehicles. Then, as if to create total impasse, temperatures plummeted to sub-zero digits. During one span of five days, temps never rallied above minus 25.

The bitter cold was what I wished was only a figment of my imagination. My career field at the time, City Manager (the equivalent of which I would never again subscribe to even my worst enemy), was exhaustively laborious. I could not with any semblance of good conscious leave our street crews out in those formidable conditions without being alongside them. They worked hard, never giving in to the elements, and honestly not even complaining. Those men personified dedication to their task and extreme concern for others to whom they owed their allegiance. In that month-long span of severely almost unimaginable weather, those men engendered my total respect and admiration.

One whole month! My wife never left the house and I actually saw her very little. When conditions changed and traveling was tolerable, we traveled all over to show off our little girl who in fact had slept through most of the malaise.

Many things cultivate my memory of that event, and all of them certainly were not bad. Of the most gratifying perhaps are the men who distinguished themselves during that time, several of whom are no longer around to talk about "the good ole times." Thankfully, we still have a few good men around today who would and <u>do</u>, do the same. There is **hope** for this great God-honored country, but integrity and dedication must be its belt buckle. That is what still holds the pants up for society.

Wouldn't it be incredible to sink this 25-footer? By the way, it is every bit as intimidating as originally perceived. Examining the

BREATHTAKING

inevitable, this putt seems to break three times before the cup would jump out and grab my ball. And was it mentioned that it is treacherously downhill and will be fast as greased lightning? Speed and length are critical and should I miss -- you reckon -- stopping the ball only a foot or two below the pin would be beautiful. Here goes! No, there it goes! And I can tell it ain't gonna' stop. It doesn't matter that it caught the left lip of the cup. That close, the ball kicked left, creating a bad angle coming back, and rolled past seven feet. What have I done? There went birdie and par now scares me to death. Why do I even play this game anyway?

Perhaps a good question would be: Why do we attempt **any**thing? The answer: *We were created for such a time as this*. Something tells me that is what Mordecai told Esther. As a result, Esther stood before the king, knowing it could be the last stand she would possibly ever take. Her stand saved her people and the victory was attributed to God, ensuing from a commitment to prayer. That is why we take hold of and grip tightly this thing called *life*. We have to try and prevail. We must! The excellency of our endeavor to be superior to failure is at stake. There can be no limit to the discharge of our effort. Losing is not an OPTION!

This is excruciating! I just missed this putt. Dismal. . . not really. It was a tap-in for bogey. Could have been a 6! Remember. . . . We are not going to sweat the small stuff and really it is **all** just small stuff. Oh, well, on to the next hole with enthusiasm. A par 3. I am going to jump all over that bad boy.

CHAPTER 7

LONG PAR 3 – UPHILL

FANTASTIC! THE SUN just broke through and the walk downhill off #6 indicates it is time to shed some clothes. You know what they say in the Bluegrass State. "If you don't like the weather right now, just wait a few minutes." What a couple of degrees of temp increase can do for one's demeanor! Certainly hope this good stuff stays around for at least twelve more holes.

Bringing the cart to a stop opposite the tee box on #7, not great thoughts are dribbling around inside that mass of stuff enclosed by the cranium. Simply put, this tee shot really gets to me. Of course I know it's coming and I'm doing my best to separate mental lapse from optimum preponderance to perform, but getting my head around this one is tough. Before even thinking of pulling a club, reaching for the rangefinder dominates first movement. For me, exact yardage from these blue tees is critical. Yeah, I know. It's a head thing.

Speaking of exact yardages, have you ever considered adding a rangefinder to your arsenal of accoutrements that makes up your vast array of golfing paraphernalia? Now I certainly don't have the latest and greatest, but in the palm of my hand is the Bushnell Tour V2, 5 X 24, laser rangefinder. This little guy has single-hand vertical operation with a selective targeting system that automatically scans, and features pinseeker mode with 5 power magnification and diopter adjustment. Unlike myself, these superlatives mean little to the nominally

LONG PAR 3 – UPHILL

adept technologist. Kidding. . . just kidding. I had a degree of difficulty reading this stuff from the box.

What I **really** want to emphasize is that this little instrument will allow you to shoot the pin and determine the precise yardage up to 300 yards. Now that is amazing! You may not have that commitment to precision -- me neither -- but this little gem is an awful lot of fun to play with. Talking about technology, Bushnell makes a rangefinder that gives you a little jolt when you are honed in on the flag. You reckon my wife might let me get one of these? Not in the near future!

Talking about critical yardage. . . . A good friend was driving to work recently and while attempting to negotiate a left turn, found himself defenseless to the undetectable icy roadway. Two hundred yards later, he encountered an embankment that had severe consequences for the Wildcat blue Ford Ranger he admires so much. Thankfully, not injured (just his ego a little out of joint), that yardage was CRITICAL for my buddy. There is an ole saying, "They make 'em every day." Hopefully, all will be okay. My point? Some things are truly critical and I'm not talking about yardage to the pin or for that matter vehicles that can be replaced. Human beings are critically relevant and our interaction with them can be devastating or world-shatteringly uplifting to them. You hold the key to communication. Even spontaneous conversation needs to be given a relative degree of thought. Superfluous, unwarranted verbal disclosures can rebuff and destroy. Knowingly meaningful remarks bring elevation to others' existence. Give some consideration to this statement from our greatest statesman: *"Be still and know that I am God."* (God) Now that is world-shattering!

172 and that's not even give or take a few. That is right on. However, this hole always plays long for me. Just a little wind but it is blowing right at me. 5 iron? Perfect! Club pulled and walking back to the tee box, the "if it can possibly happen it will" just happened. Wind not only picks up a bit straight at me, but gusts are also screaming down over the hill from right to left. Lining up several yards to the right of the pin, I mentally prepare for this shot.

LIFE IN 18 HOLES

Did I ever mention that I have just retired from full-time ministry? Blessed with a beautiful wife to encourage me and especially gifted and talented people to offer direction along the way, I have been tremendously blessed over the years. Beginning ministry bi-vocationally, I realized the struggle of balancing a full-time job with what some would call part-time pastoring. My thoughts? Pastoring is <u>never</u> part of the time! Combining the two left little time for other activities, and having enough time to spend with young children and wife was always a priority and yet very demanding. Several years full-time offered very different circumstances. Needless to say, there were still never any 40-hour weeks, and increased numbers of people simply multiplied not only the work but also the expectancy. Church people desperately need a lot of attention it seems. Not a bad thing.

Christians today seem to be dealing with excessively strong gusts of wind sweeping down from the hills of secular society. Do not misunderstand me. I do not believe those of us holding tightly to our disciplines of deeply held religious values should be exempt from criticism by those who hold other views. I have no authority to condemn them for their social behaviors nor for their strategies to reach their intended results -- nor thankfully, will I be their ultimate judge. Neither should I be condemned or denigrated for my belief in a universal God who demands my allegiance and Who, I believe, gives specific moral and social direction for the way I live and exist within today's society. We do not see things from the same periphery. That is a given.

But it astounds me that other religious beliefs seem to be given a free ride while we as Christians are blatantly attacked and lambasted for our energies to stand on biblically perceived principles. Criticisms are tolerated and certainly expected. However, attempts to alienate -- or by some to even annihilate -- beliefs based on historically sound judgment and spiritual association are preposterous.

Jesus, and the life He lived and gave for me, gives me a reason and willingness to stand for something meaningful. Elusive promises from a society torn by bitterness and despair give me little to stand

LONG PAR 3 – UPHILL

for. We need to agree to disagree and cease the destruction of one another in the process.

Confidence that this much wind will push my ball considerably to the left is essential as I settle in over this shot lined up ever so much uphill. Good solid contact and I watch as my ball gains altitude and begins to drift easily to the left, riding those strong wind currents. That was beautiful! My Pro V lands considerably right but pin high, leaving a lengthy putt but one that is totally manageable, especially given these circumstances. Hey, life is good.

Back to the cart with my enthusiasm on overload. Don't forget to put the rangefinder in its case. Slam the pedal to the metal. I feel totally unstoppable! Have you ever been that way? It seems when we get in that mode that all obstacles are completely obliterated, doubt is defused, and a sense of pressing urgency to completion wraps us within its tangle of excitement. Nothing can hinder our progress -- or at least that is the atmosphere in which we find ourselves flourishing.

As I race to the top of the hill parallel to the green, all of a sudden reality takes hold and grips me with a vengeance. The cart comes to a slow stop . . . battery is dead. I am forced to accept fact -- very reluctantly, I might add. There is nothing I can do to infuse life into this heap of mobility that was once propelling me so efficiently along this pathway to success. Uttering profanities would be the initial response of some, but come on, man! What good does that do? Changes nothing!

Stopped utterly in our tracks, rather than complain or fuss, our first mechanism of defense must be to call upon whatever medium of intervention we have at our disposal. Hey, you have a brain, don't you? USE IT! With very little thought involved, my attention turns quickly to my smart phone. Clubhouse – rescue – CALL. Simple enough. Someone will be on their way shortly to relieve me of this predicament. Even though I shouldn't, some selfish particle within me tells me to be flat-out aggravated. After all, with as few players as there are out today, you would think that no one would be sent out in a four wheeler with a low battery. Give me a break!

Then a much calmer attitude supercedes my anguish and an amazing thing known as logical thinking takes over. ALWAYS a positive thing! Face it though. We are not wired to always be logical and positive behavior seems to elude us at the most inappropriate times. Who knows? Maybe the guy in charge of carts was just having a bad day. Whatever. . . . This too shall pass. At least I am close to the green and can play this one out while the rescue mission is carried out. Lord, give me more patience, would You? I have been instructed that patience is a tremendous virtue.

Pulling the putter and heading down to the green, having plenty of time to size up this putt is actually quite refreshing. Maybe my difficulties, as the ole saying goes, were "just meant to be." Hey, man, stop to think of all the stuff that is going on in your life right now. Some things you simply can't control and some you probably wouldn't need to even if you could. Others possibly have been laid in your path as a means of enunciating, "Slow down!" Take some time to get a good grip on your surroundings. Step up alongside of reality and understand that in all circumstances it is not intended for us to be in charge. Our mental extremities must be energized to allow us to understand when to take charge and also when it is time for us to completely **back off**. Part of being human is accepting we do have some imperfections, and that occasionally those personal impurities can come back to bite us if we attempt to **force** our will on circumstances we have no right to attach ourselves to.

No severe break in this putt as I was fearful there could be. A long, consistent turn slightly downhill appears to invest itself in a copious line funneling directly into the cup. Now if only the obvious can be achieved. Plenty of time to garner all the calm and concentration needed (still no hint of my rescue cart coming). Allow the shoulders to glide freely and gaze eagerly at the results . . . all that is needed. Contact. Not bragging, but that was perfect.

Excitement grips me as my eyes race behind the Pro V on what appears to be a magnetically drawn curvature that is destined for the bottom of the cup. Only a few more feet of what is perfect line

LONG PAR 3 – UPHILL

and hopes of no unseen divots that will dissuade the ball from its destination.

What a beautiful sound! I mentioned it earlier -- that indescribable "plop" as the ball makes contact with the bottom of that plastic masterpiece called the *cup*. YES! Retrieving the ball and replacing the pin, can't resist giving the ball a kiss. You tell me. Why in the world would we have the audacity to do that?

Looking back up the cart path, I distinguish the tell-tale sound of deliverance on its way. Big smile on his face, Jimmy comes to a screeching halt behind my loaded but defunct cart. Close on his heels, Cramer comes flying onto the scene. First words -- almost simultaneously from both -- "How's your game?" Reply. . . "Not bad. Not bad at all." Good friends, those guys. They quickly help me change out my stuff to the charged-up cart, hook to the dead one for its retrieval back to the barn, and send me on my way with a few nuances that are just those guys. Had minor troubles not beset me, I may have hurried that putt and missed. Who knows? Making that birdie sure was an exceptional feeling. And you know what? Nothing was ever mentioned of the dilemma with the out-of-commission cart. When all is said and done, NO BIGGIE!

Good friends though, that is a BIG deal. Having talked about this subject earlier, the importance of really good friends is truly an endowment. Being there for someone, even though it may not be game-changing, goes without telling. But, oh, when it really matters, its significance is transforming. I can never overemphasize the brilliance of friendship and will possibly mention it again before these eighteen holes are played.

The camaraderie felt, the made-birdie, and just the sheer bliss of being on the course today have totally taken all thought away from the next hurdle about to be faced. Number 8. Number One handicap hole on the course. As I listen to the hum of the tires on the cart path, reality springs into its profound magnitude, and a little gut-gnawing transcends the obvious. This hole is pretty tough. I mean, I hardly ever par this bad boy.

CHAPTER **8**

NUMBER 1 HANDICAP

BRUTAL, I'M THINKING. . . rolling to a stop right alongside the blue tees on #8. I have an almost love/hate relationship with this hole. Do you get any feeling for this? Layout is absolutely beautiful, plenty enough room to work my shot, yet I can never seem to score well. The green is guarded, but only one small bunker ever seems to come into play and it is not too difficult to stay away from. Off the tee creates no great alarm. And played halfway decently, you are not left with severe above or below the feet lies. So what's the problem? Good question? You tell me! Could it be that this has been designated the Number1 handicap (degree of difficulty) hole on the course? Let me tell you. This designed piece of mastery of available terrain certainly exposes itself as a proverbial headscratcher.

Now understandably, some of you are absolute gurus when it comes to the nomenclature attached to the different aspects of the golf game , while others play yet know hardly anything about rules, etc. In other words, some take this stuff seriously, and others could care less as long as you get to hit that little round ball and then chase after it in sheer desperation. As a result, perhaps I should give explanation to what is probably one of the least thought about aspects of the game: the *hole* handicap or degree of difficulty for a particular hole. After all, the chapter title lends credence to it.

Each hole on every golf course is assigned a number or level of

NUMBER 1 HANDICAP

difficulty rating from 1 to 18. Supposedly, the most difficult hole to play is saddled with a #1 handicap while the least has a #18 hung on it. While two or more people are playing a match, the golfer with the higher handicap is given strokes (*handicap strokes*) by the more proficient player or lower handicap. We could call that "leveling the playing field." Strokes given equal the difference between the high handicapper and the one with the lower handicap. Example: Player with a 14 handicap receives 7 strokes from his opponent wielding a 7 handicap. But how or on what hole is the stroke given? This is where the *hole* handicap comes in.

When my buddy S.R. and I are playing a grudge match and reluctantly I am required to give him 9 strokes, we first analyze the scorecard. We determine the first 9 handicap holes and S.R. gets a stroke on each of those holes. Again, example: We tee it up on #1, this being designated a #7 handicap hole, and S.R. receives a stroke. When we tee off on #2, *hole* being designated a 13 handicap, we are playing straight up. S.R. receives no special privileges. (He doesn't deserve anything anyway!) When the match is over, he has cheated me (just kidding) out of 9 total strokes and I had better have beaten him by 10 or more strokes to win the match.

Allow me to interject another small morsel of information. The hole with the designation of Number 1 handicap hole on the course may very well not be the most difficult to play. This is the kicker. . . the Number 1 handicap hole is the one where the higher handicap player is most likely to need a stroke for an equalizer. If the low handicap golfer is just as likely to make bogey as the high handicapper, a stroke is not needed or warranted. Of necessity, the determining group responsible for establishing hole handicaps for a particular course is saddled with this endeavor. Far beyond me! I must say, however, #8 that I am standing on now seems to give more people more grievance than any other hole on this course. Substantial call by the handicapper, I would presume. Much more discussion could be had on this subject. For instance, how you might even be given 2 strokes on a particular hole. But. . . enough confusion already. Let's beat this dead horse no more!

Teeing off from this box is awesome! The green is not in the player's line of sight, slight dogleg left; however, a landing area just shy of the 150- yard marker is flat as a tabletop. This sets you up for a very "go for it" second shot. One problem. Have you ever noticed how little hard round balls seem to have an aversion for tabletops? Miss to the left and you will be standing way above your ball -- if you can even find it in the rough stuff -- calculating what your second shot should be. To the right is cart path. You know you don't want to encounter that critter. And a little more right and you are lavished with timber and undergrowth designated out of bounds. Fortunately, a good drive flying off the head of my Callaway driver has left me not exactly perfect, a little short perhaps, but this green will be doable in two.

Negotiating a couple of turns on the cart path, my momentum slows to a halt directly across from my ball which found the fairway. Quite a distance away with no carts allowed on this fairway today necessitates walking over to check out the lie and club needed for this approach shot. Back to the cart and back again. Oh, well. Through all this necessary maneuvering, handicap keeps permeating my thoughts. *Handicap* by definition means a condition that markedly restricts a person's ability to function physically, mentally, or socially. In other words, factors regardless of what they are which hinder us or limit us would be considered handicaps.

Many folks are born with very limiting encumbrances, many of which can never be outdistanced. Our best efforts for those mentally and physically exposed from birth can only be to draw them up close in prayer and trust a much greater Authority to nurture and sustain. Handicap due to accident or war would fall into this same arena of concern. Other forms of handicap are manageable or even leave us with the proclivity to overcome. One such handicap that I personally believe many suffer from and eventually succumb to is the inability to free themselves from what they believe others perceive them to be or the detrimental nature of thoughts others have toward them. This is

NUMBER 1 HANDICAP

a self-imposed handicap and one that **can** and **must** be totally eradicated. Overpowering and belittling, continued self-exposure to such a restrictive -- albeit completely unnecessary -- disability lends itself to radically uncompromising results. Deprivating as this uncensored condition may be, total beat-down of any expression that tends to give credence to such abnormalities must occur.

Man must realize that he was not created in the image of God to be relegated to negative status by the pernicious actions of his fellow man. Not saying this is an everyday happening. But critically demoralizing emergences are often the result of self-imposed perception. This is never initialized amidst the realm of the positive, self-elevated, and creatively mature thinker. This is indentured servant mentality. We must rise above mental debt-bondage illusions and soar with incredible inclination to overcome.

Another limitation, *handicap* if you will, is our own physical inability to perform in certain areas. We all have them. And yet we often allow what are actually minor infirmities to defer our accomplishments in an unmitigated way. Hey, man, we are not all going to perform like Tiger or Phil. We may never peruse intellectual altitudes like an Einstein. The likes of Mother Teresa or Billy Graham may never be in the offing for us. Listen closely if you will to a thought given me by a power completely outside of me: "We never know what our limits are until we attempt to push past them!" This, with no doubt, takes an overlooking of the conditions surrounding us.

One man who has pre-empted and changed my life forever said: *"Not my will but T*hy will." Jesus was in the garden talking to his Father, suffering through tremendous mental, emotional, and — what would soon be -- physical distress. This turning loose allowed him to press on. . . pressing on to results that have liberated my life and if not yours already, can and will. Another remarkable man that has impacted the lives of millions, Saul of Tarsus, known to us as Paul, suffered from what he termed a *"thorn in the flesh."* Handicap! After pleading with God three times to remove it from him, he relied upon the affirmation of Jesus: *"My grace is sufficient for you, for My strength is*

LIFE IN 18 HOLES

made perfect in weakness."

Never allow something or someone either outside you or inside you to weaken or kill your determination to be the best, whatever it is, that you can be. Push past your limits or at least . . . give it a shot!

As mentioned earlier, the ball is setting up pretty well, leaving a good lie. Why not try a new club recently purchased, a 5 Rescue, the V4 made by Adams? According to the rangefinder, 185 to the pin and as notoriously per usual, pin placement is tough today. But when is it not? Having hit this club sparingly, good solid contact as a result of a smooth swing is what I'm looking for. Keep your head down and steady, eyes on the ball, and execute. Nothing to it. Right? I wish! Remarkably, everything worked as planned and watching the Pro V settle down on the green is exhilarating. Can't see the back side of the green, know it's past the pin, but hoping it hasn't run off the putting surface. I'm satisfied.

Rescue. . . seems a funny name to call a golf club, doesn't it? Well, that certainly wasn't my idea but I really like the club. Well-balanced for optimum performance, the ball seems to rapidly accelerate off the club face. But *rescue?* Eliminating the thought of golf for a moment, life seems to deal out situations from time to time that leave me in need of rescue. Not so much life in general, but particular areas of life that are a result of self-generated predicaments. Overzealous ambition or intolerant inactions often find me in need of a Savior. Ever happen to you? I openly admonish aggressive behavior and determination; however, be constantly aware of the feelings of those who encircle your domain.

Never purposefully, I have the tendency to hurt (not physically) the dearest creature on earth to me, my wife. I retaliate, of course, and explain to her that she is just too sensitive, knowing all along that it is simply a dubious exertion lending no relevance to what should not even be an argument. After manly ego departs and humiliation takes its order, getting away to my secret place and negotiating the results with my heavenly Father, seems I always come out on the short end of the stick. Grace prevails and embarrassment exudes. It

NUMBER 1 HANDICAP

is desperately time for RESCUE! Get my drift? Knowingly, there are lots of rescue situations we could discuss. Actually, life rescue, as a consequence of our own indulgences, permeates the atmosphere of necessity. Stop to think. Not physically -- but mentally, emotionally, and spiritually -- how do **you** find reconciliation? Go to your source, the Creator of the creature you are, and search out some avenues of guilt elimination. Makes a difference and feels better every time.

Racing the cart onto the small cul-de-sac of the cart path, peripheral vision illuminates a small white object nestled in the extra thick grass just off the right, back of the green. What I was hoping didn't. . . did. Leaving a very delicate chip onto a steep slope that if carried too far is going to run the ball way beyond the pin. Using a sand wedge, my effort to barely pop the ball up and land it on the fringe did not materialize. Not much but a shade too long. And I watch that little ball of energy pick up speed and race past the pin, coming to stop on a precarious break line about 12 to 15 feet beyond my intended objective.

Standing over this putt and staring it down with a resolve that would put Tom Watson to shame, the break seems impossible to read. Kind of like life, you say. Sometimes at the fork in the road it is indeterminable which direction will find itself in compliance with what needs to be a lucrative decision. Trusting and relying on divine providence -- historically having hopefully made similar decisions based on sought-after facts and perhaps advice from a proven comrade -- put your best inclination into gear and ride it home to success. There is that aggressive nature again and you may even make a few mistakes occasionally. However, never depart from interstate thinking that fuels instinct and determination. Winding country road mentality extends itself to relaxed vacation type thinking, but never to profound propulsion into an exuberant future. High octane is the way to go! Just remember to prepare for the extra cost.

Can't tell. Seems to break right before suffering from two other breaks before reaching the pin. At least the last breaks are easy to see and it is all uphill. Have to hit it hard enough and trust your gut. What else is new? On its way, not bad, left it a couple of turns short – well, about two feet. But I am good with that. Tapping this short putt in leaves me with bogey and kind of irritated that seldom do I make par on this hole. One thing to strive for though. I have never birdied this Number 1 handicap. Reminds me of what Jim Valvano said: "Never give up."

Back in the cart and it's up the steep hill to the tee box. Number 9 is what I would call the "transition hole" as it seems to set you up for the back nine. I really like this one. So settle in, my friends. Time to negotiate this "easy par 4."

CHAPTER 9

EASY PAR 4

ONE UNDER GOING into #9. Not too shabby for me. No one could ask for a better setup or transition hole to kick off the back nine. Good straight drive up the middle or even a little to the right lends itself to a short second shot to this huge green that can get a little fast coming off the top, but nothing that is not manageable.

Caution. Don't go left! Steep embankment, lots of junk, and might I add . . . out of bounds. Should you be on the fairway left, mature trees guard the approach hiding the left side of the green. Possible to get over them, but not the easiest situation to negotiate if pin placement is dead left. Albeit plenty of green to work with and an excellent view of the club house that awaits that relaxing intermission which appropriately gets you ready for the challenge of another nine.

This really is the perfect transition hole. Now if you google the word *transition*, you find: the process or a period of changing from one state or condition to another. Literally, this may not be the most effective use of the word for this situation, but to me it is the perfect fit. When playing the game of golf, always do we refer to playing the front nine and the back nine which sensibly indicates there is a difference or a change. The game is a process so we are attempting to maneuver our way through what usually will be two totally different conditions on the course, front and back nine. Seems like a remarkable explanation to me and only remotely not understandable. I am

◄ **LIFE IN 18 HOLES**

totally aware that many are not unequivocally emboldened to such depth of maturity of understanding. Joke. . . get it?

Seriously, transition is a time of unobstructed preparation. In life we constantly experience change by simply living through the process. Then there are those times of more serious departure from the norm and we must find ourselves mentally, physically, and emotionally equipped to innovate or even perhaps manipulate our way to favorable advantage in this precarious structure known as *life*. Probably a bad time to interject this thought. . . . It is kind of like walking up on the tee box and teeing the ball up next to the marker that is the least distance from your cart. To be honest, that is just plain ole laziness! Visualize the shot just as you should visualize and analyze an important change in life that no doubt will impact your very existence for an awfully long time. On the tee box, take some time to see where the DANGER lies on that particular hole. Then tee up left, right, or middle . . . whichever allows you optimum exposure or the most fairway available to you away from trouble. Life transitions are very much like the tee box. Don't line up your shot at life where failure is staring you straight in the face. Steer away from it, minimize your risks, and never be lulled into failing situations as a result of what seem to be quick fixes or "can't miss" opportunities. Trust me. Murphy's law is a reality and there are no easy outs when you are negotiating life's process.

Several years ago while still in the work force and actively engaged in sales, I received a call from what seemed to be the most unlikely potential customer. One thing about sales: Never underestimate the presumed impossible. On the opposite end of the conversation was the COO of a dog track and casino.

To help you understand this divergent situation, I sold automotive equipment and the two totally unrelated situations seemed to have no realistic relation. Obviously, she was completely in control of her motive and I was abruptly invited into the equation. Equation: These folks were advertisement-driven. As part of their myriad of promotions, high-end sports cars were given away. (Of course there was always a "small" fee involved.)

Thus, they were in the market for a lift to afford them the option of raising those gems high above their clientele, creating exquisite exposure. I just happened to sell the best lift or automotive rack on the market and they were well aware of that. Plus, the potential to design, build, and install a lift to highlight their ingenious ambitions was at my disposal.

Walking into that particular appointment understandably was somewhat different than usual. Immediately catching my eye was a brilliant red corvette, stunningly displayed, and it didn't take long to decipher that intentions for a meticulously placed lift was right there. I was approached by a security guard who informed me to wait at that particular spot. Surveying the area, I began to put together a plan that I felt would enhance ultimate exposure. On cue, a young lady introduced herself as the person in charge and we eventually came to an agreement that seemed very attractive for each of us. DEAL!

I have to tell you, I had never been in an atmosphere such as that before. Slot machines were positioned everywhere and people were standing in line to await their turn at immediate wealth. Unfortunately, what I witnessed was quite to the contrary. I am assuming, hard-earned money was being shoved into those machines, and I heard very few bells and whistles go off as the result of someone hitting a jackpot. Kind of sad, don't you think? Instant gratification is what it is all about. Let me tell you something. That place could not afford a very high-priced lift to show off a very expensive car that they had to purchase if everyone playing walked away a winner. Common sense. But how much of that is used anymore?

While there, I watched the greyhounds run. Something else I had never experienced before. Those dogs, chasing a fake rabbit controlled by an operator in an undisclosed place taunting them to exert themselves to complete exhaustion, ran with only one thing in mind and that was to catch that rabbit. Poor critters -- oblivious to the fact that someone was possibly throwing away their last dollar just to see if they could pick a winner -- were busting themselves to catch

LIFE IN 18 HOLES

something that would always be elusive.

Hey, guys, so many people are doing the same things in so many different venues and constantly coming up short just like the ones at the dog track. Some would say they are chasing their dream or labeling it in some other fashion to dispense of responsibility, but I really don't believe such actions could ever be considered sound financial planning. Far-fetched, woefully elusive, and misled ambitions are often bred out of a mentality of entitlement. To these I would say. . . educate yourselves against such infirmities and equip yourselves to be overcomers of the maladies that await the precariously uninformed.

Adding one more trivial injection into my total departure of the "easy par 4", I must remind you that Kentucky is the breeding place of my very existence. Without explanation, the Commonwealth is the horse capital of the world and the "Bluegrass" hosts THE most watched sports spectacular, the *Kentucky Derby*. Churchill Downs is a marvelous setting located in Louisville and displays all the entrapments that allure the rich and famous. Another great venue, home of the *Rolex Kentucky,* is the Kentucky Horse Park located just outside of Lexington at Georgetown, KY. The Kentucky thoroughbred, famous for its racing prowess, is a magnificent animal, gorgeous to look at, and entrenched with a competitive nature that is unbelievable. This marvelous creature, after making the turn and heading down the stretch in any race, is such a competitor that *give up* is not an option. And each one would "run itself into the ground" before allowing another four-legged animal to overtake its domain of supremacy.

If human athletes could drive themselves to the limits of the thoroughbred or the greyhound, world class results would be exhilarating. However, physical results would be institutionalizing. Strangely enough, we really need the intensity, tenacity, and fortitude of world class performers as we indulge in this game of *life* and struggle against the liability of mediocrity. We must have our "A" game. Granted, in the game of golf, most of us are not earning our living or supporting a family from the proceeds. But why play if you do not want to compete? Same in life. Never rely on hitting the elusive big lick or wallow in the

EASY PAR 4

filth of what could have been if only you were luckier. That word *lucky*. . . simply eradicate it from your vocabulary and begin to create self-gratification that results from a positive and aggressive nature.

Slots, following the horses or the dogs, all seem to accentuate a complex allurement in some folks, separating itself into uncontrollable compulsion . . . GAMBLING! Certainly not a good vocation for the average to pursue, but we all have been guilty of winning at something once and finding ourselves obsessed with the "can't wait" perception that I must try again.

Let me tell you. One extremely good swing of the club that results in a much better than average result is what makes golf so addicting and intensifies that insatiable desire to do it again. Number 9 is also that kind of hole. Its layout is perfect -- a scoring dream even for the less than average golfer -- gets you stoked to make the turn, and is simply a lot of fun. I guess if you were ever driven to golf obsession, this hole would "rachet up" the ante in a heartbeat.

Coming to a stop adjacent to the tee box, you can hardly wait to tee it up especially when you have a pretty good round going. Teeing away from trouble. . . remember? Concentration takes center stage. Actually, this is a very easy driving hole; however, do not plan that approach to the green before successfully getting off the tee. This is really one of those "I can't wait to hit it again" holes. Right up the middle. Man, that was good! And I am left with a 9 iron into a pin placement that is begging you to hit it close. If I were a gambler, I would almost bet on a birdie to close out the front nine. But first things first!

Heading up the cart path, I can't help thinking about how blessed I am and have been. No longer do I have opportunity to hunt or fish with my son, but when we get together and weather permits, golf separates itself from the rest of the field. My son-in-law makes it a threesome whenever possible. Hey, man, that is good stuff.

Then there are friends like S.R. and others who really add to the dimensions of life as we know it. Mutual trust and friendship are so important in this world where people are always watching their back and fearful of what is coming next.

LIFE IN 18 HOLES

Jesus said *He was giving us His peace and leaving that peace with us*. On this ride through life we will never be totally free of turbulence, but knowing the ONE who speaks to those forces and says *"Be still"* takes out the angst. Embrace family and friends, and know that the God of the universe will never leave or forsake you.

Anxious to hit this shot with 9 iron in hand, I realize this ball must be struck cleanly and I don't want to take anything off it. Visualizing this shot, the ball hits a few feet past the hole with spin that draws it back leaving a short uphill putt. Now to pull that off . . . . PERFECT! Just a tap-in for birdie. Walking up on # 9 under these conditions doesn't get much better. Can't help thinking: A really good friend would give me this one.

What a day so far! Two under through nine and momentum heading to the back nine. You know, momentum is huge. We need it in golf and we need it in life. Momentum is a producer and it challenges us to wring out every drop of effort and ingenuity that exists somewhere within us. It pumps us for the next thing -- whatever that thing is -- and creates an atmosphere of winning. Momentum is never a "shell" game because we are so sure of what the next move is that we are never searching for the pea. It counteracts that which is negative and elevates performance that supercedes any recognition of mediocrity. Flat out -- it is the gear that transfers unrealized power to the back axle of our lives and blows all competition away as we come off the starting line smokin'. "Big Mo" equates to stuff realized but never thought possible. Search for it – create it – do something – but get it! It is a life changer!

Back in the cart, I am all out to make the turn. Something about a good score that keeps you pushing. Kind of like education. Good grades lead to good scholarships which lead to good jobs which lead to successful lives. Hey, guys, challenge your kids to excel in school -- not expecting more than should be expected -- but never allowing them to settle for less than is attainable. You owe them that . . . that is what love does for them.

Man, I wish nature weren't calling!

CHAPTER **10**

DON'T GET ANY STRAIGHTER THAN THIS

STANDING BEHIND THE ball . . . visualizing the shot . . . hey! I can see my garage door from this tee box -- never realized that before. Wondering. . . . How many things in life simply go unnoticed? And not just immaterial things like I just experienced, but things of consequence. Like the creation of the Creator. Have I noticed it lately? Someone in need. Have I impacted their life? Encouragement. Have I given my family any today? Health. Am I taking care of mine? Thoughts. Are mine under control? Spirituality. How is my relationship with "The Man Upstairs"? And on and on. . . but you get the picture. Some things are of absolute importance and should demand our attention unequivocally. While others, not so much. So why do they always seem to meddle with and infiltrate unnecessarily our train of thought? Could it be lack of control?

Speaking of control, sizing up my tee shot on 10, have I given complete attention to my pre-shot routine? Some of you guys who just want to hit the ball and chase it (and really that is beautiful) are probably thinking, "What the heck is a pre-shot routine?" Well, watch any PGA tournament and pay particular attention to any one pro and follow his every shot. The routine from address to follow through is always the same. It is so unvaried that when watching some of those

◄ LIFE IN 18 HOLES

guys, Keegan Bradley for instance, it just about wears you out.

Just think. . . . As a result of that repetition, most of those guys are NOT financially challenged. Get it? Could that mean that possibly I should attempt to emulate some of those practices? Might just work for you, too. If you can't establish a good routine, ask for some advice. I guarantee you that someone will jump all over the opportunity to unleash upon you their vast array of usually unsought-afte, professional-like wisdom.

Life . . . . Could there be such a thing as doing a few of those get-you-to-successful-places repetitions before you jump through the next hoop? Solid foundations of advancement are always laid the same way. You don't need to reinvent the wheel! Take a block layer for example. He always starts with a sturdy, reliable corner and lays each block along a straight line using exact repetitive actions. But keep in mind, no block is laid until a solid foundation has been established. Do what it takes to establish an exceptional *life* foundation and then never deviate from the what-got-you-there repetitions in all your future endeavors. Do that and you will be okay! Call it life's next pre-shot routine, if you want.

This is a great back nine starter . . . straight as a stick. But careful! It will jump up and bite you. The middle is wide open but tall rough and trees line the right side with some sand mingled in. To the left it gets steep, and a ball over there could wind up on #18 fairway. Simple enough – hit it straight! After that solid, straight drive, stay out of the sand that fronts the green on both sides and this hole is a piece of cake. Easier said than done, my friend.

Really, this is not a difficult hole to execute, but as the ole saying goes, "looks are deceiving", and the tendency to not concentrate results. Remember. This is a game of concentration. You can't afford to think of that difficult hole coming up and lose focus on what is at hand. How many of you are Bible readers? Do you recall the walking-on-water story? What we encounter in this episode is a classic example of lack of concentration. Peter, in his exuberance to go to Jesus, stayed afloat so to speak, as long as his attention was not

DON'T GET ANY STRAIGHTER THAN THIS

diverted from his intended goal. But immediately upon losing focus with attention misdirected toward the wind and the waves, his buoyancy was completely diminished and he began to sink. Peter was afraid, we are told, because he lost concentration on his only source of subsistence and he cried out for help. By the way, his SOURCE came through!

In this game of life that we all have to direct our attention toward, we must be focused and maintain our concentration. There will always be obstructions that circumvent our abilities to maneuver with confidence and keep ourselves atop the waves. The winds of disobedience to meticulous detail of excellence will never cease to blow across the bow of our mainframe. Concentration on our source of provision and dependency upon our allegiance to Him will enable us to flee the turbulence of distraction and overcome the despondency that comes from a lack of it. Lack of concentration clouds our view of the end goal. Total focus and commitment to every facet of each endeavor illuminate that to which we are destined. Without it, we walk in darkness, and in darkness we cannot determine where we are going. Walk in the light and believe!

Overcoming the distraction of my garage door, total attention to the task at hand is imperative. Down the middle is my focus and just beyond that, black and white stake (150-yard marker) would be perfect. Let's do it!

Ball teed pretty low, trying to keep it down out of a pretty stiff wind coming out of the west. I approach the ball. Placing the ball a little farther back in my stance than usual and attempting to hit through it rather than lift it off the tee, backswing is smooth with a nice follow through resulting in my ball getting good roll and checking up just left of middle with expected distance. Is it not always good to achieve your anticipated results?

As I hop up into the cart, I can't help but think of a couple of guys I play with fairly often. Rick hits driver fairly well. And Bill. . . well, Bill hits driver all the time. It doesn't matter if it's a short par 3 that I might pull out a wedge on or a 600-yard par 5. Bill hits driver.

LIFE IN 18 HOLES

Great thing is, it seems to work for him. Those two guys always ride together, and S.R. (you remember S.R.) and I ride the same cart. We have a super time! Never pay much attention to etiquette, have been known to break a rule or two -- but it is always fun. Life needs to be fun! Be competitive, be a producer, never fail to pay attention to detail, but always have fun. Our time here on this ole earth is just too short not to.

Rolling to a stop for my second, I knew what I was going to pull from the bag well before getting here. You know, life is so much simpler when we plan well in advance of our next move, or we are so on top of our game that the next action we take is a no-brainer. Call it preparation or planning ahead or whatever, being ready to move when opportunity presents itself is awesome. Part of being in that attack mode is always recognizing how your action and the outcome will affect the lives of those around you. My wife and I were having breakfast in a fun little restaurant not long ago, when conversation with our server stirred a thought process in me I will never forget. Kerry had a very minor request of the young man that was met with a most profound response: "If it's important to you, it's important to me." Needless to say, his tip was far above average. We learned he was working his way through school, but I believe he already had his heels dug in solidly to a pattern of behavior that will lead to undaunted success. So I learned, and hope I never fail to apply, this simple motivational tool: "If it's important to you, it's important to me." Unbelievable outcomes will erode from that message.

Pulling that pre-planned club (8 iron) and again positioning the ball in my stance so its trajectory would penetrate the stiff wind rather than ride high and get knocked down by the wind, I could see that Pro V settling down on the front of the green and rolling out for a short uphill putt. Position and setup over the ball were critical to a good shot and fortunately, everything was working well on this one.

Golf shots are always important, right? But putting yourself in position to not get knocked down by life's stuff is crucial. Proper positioning, be it legal, ethical, or moral (and might I add common-sensible),

DON'T GET ANY STRAIGHTER THAN THIS

will increase personal viability in the workplace and merit its occupant with a treasure trove of accomplishment.

I will take that shot any day! Eight feet straight uphill with little-to-no break and all I have to do is hit it firm. You know. . . just thought of a tremendous difference in the game of golf and the game we play called *life*. On the putting green, we would always settle for a straight putt with no breaks. In life, we are always looking for those good breaks.

Now I wonder. . . who concocted that great euphemism? A *break* usually denotes an undesirable interlude, such as: I broke my arm or I broke the plate. Breaks usually indicate the need for repair rather than the intriguing awakening of success. Nonetheless, big breaks in life are sought after and due diligence seems to be the predecessor of receiving one. Whatever. . . . Honestly though, I hope you get yours if you've worked hard for it. Just had another astonishing thought! Something we say all the time that means little: "Give me a break!"

Sure, said it before, but this deserves repeating. Such a wonderful sound when that Pro V hits the bottom of the cup. Just made that putt for birdie. Three under after 10. I can't believe this round today! Life and thrills associated with it do shock us sometimes.

Stop signs are usually erected to caution us that imminent risk could be looming and we need to be careful. Right? But sometimes we humans show our inability to reason sensibly and ignore obvious declarations of potential catastrophe which lead to otherwise avoidable bodily harm. To put it bluntly -- STUPID! But whoever said that *homosapien* indicates intellect that is always geared toward critical reason? After all, the urban dictionary gives the definition of *homosapien* (human) as, "A pitiful race that will most likely cause its own extinction before its technologies fully develop." Said all that to say this. Leaving #10 green and back in that NASCAR-like golf cart, you are immediately confronted with a stop sign that indicates you are about to cross the main street in this entire complex. Silver Lake Drive is a very wide thoroughfare visited regularly by obviously distracted drivers. They are oblivious to being on the planet, approaching

LIFE IN 18 HOLES

breakneck speeds. Thus, good reason for a stop sign to warn the overindulgent golfer. Unfortunately, these golfers around here are totally inept of logically thinking, ignoring all signs of common reason including STOP signs, and creating the potential for very disastrous results. Fortunately, close calls are all I have heard of so far.

Just a word to the wise: Stop signs, RR crossing signs, crosswalks, deer crossing signs, BURMA SHAVE signs (Have you seen them?) -- all of these have been placed at critical junctures for obvious reasons. HEED them! By following these well-intentioned indicators, you may live another day and may even be rewarded with another round of golf.

Drive safe through this intersection and let's play #11. . .

CHAPTER 11

I CAN'T SEE THE GREEN

CROSSING THE ROAD and winding around to the tee box on #11, a wide fairway with a fairly steep hill awaits the golfer. Actually, the hill is high enough to ward off any view of the large green which is surrounded with bunkers. Some sand on either side of the fairway at the top of the hill hardly ever causes any problem. Esthetic value is pretty good though. A good tee shot to the top of the hill opens the possibility of a lot of roll down the other side and a decent second shot. Come up short off the tee and you are looking at a long approach to the green and still possibly no view of the pin. All in all, this is a great hole. But trouble lurks all the way to the pin if shots are not well planned and executed properly.

Executed properly. . . . This can actually be a very broad statement applied to almost anything you can imagine. Do not most things in life loaded up with any degree of significance require this kind of treatment? For example, the alignment of your car. Proper alignment means less tire wear and longevity for the entire front end of your vehicle, but we seldom think about it. However, when the need arises, a trained technician needs to execute the procedure flawlessly. We never like to dole out the $79.75 (arbitrary figure but close). It pays in the long run though. Tires, ball joints, and all those other parts up front are expensive when replacement is required, so seeking out an expert to execute this task properly is a money saver. Money saving should be a big time, well planned, and properly executed activity in your life. What's in your wallet?

Speaking of money, golf can be a pretty pricy activity to get involved in. Clubs, a golf bag, balls, and all the other "we think absolutely necessary" essentials that go into playing this game can get totally out there. Green fees . . . well, that's another story. Being an average player with average financial capabilities, it is necessary for me to seek out courses that are affordable yet offer excellent esthetic value and challenge suitable to my game. My wife and I were recently in Hilton Head, SC visiting some friends who were there for the winter, and we played a couple of rounds at courses we could afford. At the famous course with the beautiful lighthouse where a PGA tour event is held each year and the public can play, green fees were so far north of my wallet that I won't even mention the dollar amount. Did go look!

Membership certainly can have its advantages, especially if you have opportunity to play frequently. But get a grip! Joining for the prestige is a dumb move and many clubs have amenities you are required to pay for whether or not you use them. Okay if you have more money than good sense. Let's face it. Most of us are not in that category and value becomes the most important issue. Old Silo is a beautiful and challenging course with relatively good membership rates. VIP membership is pretty unique in that for a very low yearly fee, VIPers can play almost any time for an additional per-round fee which is very reasonable and includes cart. This is very attractive, especially if you enjoy playing other courses. I feel full membership here would kind of tie me here, making me feel fiscally irresponsible if I played other courses. Golf is a great game and splurging occasionally is like stopping at DQ for a blizzard -- the large size with extra toppings -- but don't make it a habit. Neither physically nor fiscally is it worth it. Seek out the good deals and they **are** out there. That's smart golf.

Standing behind my ball and visually picturing my down-the-middle shot, there are several objects to use as an aiming point but

I CAN'T SEE THE GREEN

one in particular stands out. A very large house with a huge upstairs window is directly behind this green that is out of your line of sight. Concentrating on that window, I can just see the perfect shot with a little draw, landing just beyond the crest of the hill and taking off. What I have to be careful of is coming out of my swing and pushing the ball right. I can still get enough distance, but the potertial for a good second can really get bad with some rough terrain up there. Focus. . . concentration. . . name of the game. And all will be well. Good mechanics result in a good shot, but distance comes up a little short of the top of the hill. Oh, well, middle of the fairway with an excellent lie looking down on this green is a result I can live with. Big factor in getting my desired result was the good aiming point. Always pick out that spot that will allow for optimum ball flight and concentrate on it, especially if you are sizing up a shot on that totally out-of-sight target.

Driver back in bag. Breakneck speed down over the steep hill is of necessity. Right? WRONG! Usually we are so bent on getting to that next shot, especially if the last one left you in good shape, we don't pay a lot of attention to what we are doing. Everyone knows etiquette is a big thing in golf, but did you ever stop to think that safety may just be a big issue also?

Unfortunately, we are not always guilty of THINKING. Every new year on the course seems to bring the same old stories of riders thrown from the cart, carts off the cart path on those hairpin turns, or carts being pulled out of a creek. These are just a few examples of the carnage that occurs as a result of totally inexcusable safety practices.

There is also the issue of drinking and driving which is illegal on our highways and in my opinion, should be illegal on our cart paths. Now I know a lot of guys who have their little coolers and for them a beverage or two is just normal during the round. But it seems there are those who have way more than a couple and not only can they become obnoxious to other players, but safety for themselves and others becomes a huge issue. Often with company outings, some who are out there could care less about the golf but really get into the free drinks and fun with their buddies. *Dangerous* would be a loose term to apply to these situations that develop and increase in intensity as the day goes on. Safety, destruction of property, and no telling what else may result.

Now I know "stuff" happens regardless of how careful we may be. Just remember. Safety is a big issue. Pay attention to the conditions around you, drive safely, be respectful of others on the course who paid their green fees just like you did, and don't spoil an otherwise beautiful experience called *life* that you have been blessed with.

Having negotiated the hills safely, I pull alongside my ball that is setting up perfectly. Not only can I now see the green, but the pin placement is perfect: a little forward of and center of that beautifully manicured piece of landscape called the putting surface. For the first-timer on this course, wondering where you are off the tee is a bit intimidating. However, when you top the hill and look down on this gorgeous green surrounded by beautiful homes and nature's features, you are more than glad you came to play.

Still, problems can bite you on this second shot. To be honest, I should always just lay up to the front of the green, eliminate any exposure to several bunkers surrounding it, and leave myself with a short pitch and run for an easy par. To be quite honest, doing what I should do while playing this ridiculously addicting game has not always been one of my finer points.

Challenge is always intriguing to me. To be quite honest, I think it should be. However, common sense should be a prerogative sought after, especially in critical situations you find yourself in. . . in life. The hype or mystique surrounding a particular situation often throws us over the top when considering our *modus operandi*. The actions we choose are often a result of the glamour or excitement involved rather than the detailed, calculated maneuvers obvious to sound judgment and experience. Yet there is that cavalier nature that needs to be satisfied. So occasionally, life -- just like golf -- needs to be experimented with and tweaked a little bit. It does pay, however, to not be extraneous in your thinking. Know your parameters. To put it bluntly, think smart!

I CAN'T SEE THE GREEN

Everything is perfect. Got to go for it. Five iron should be dead on. A little breeze in my face, but the distance is great for this club and I really enjoy hitting the five. Seems strange maybe, but there are clubs we feel very comfortable hitting while others we kind of dread pulling. "Head thing", I believe, but nonetheless true. Line this one up for a little draw, leaving it on the front edge with a good roll, and I should be home free. All I have to do is execute. Good contact -- it didn't move! Straight as could be but I didn't get the draw. Guess you know what that means . . . bunker to the right. And I have never been the world's greatest out-of-the-sand.

Well, the drive down over this picturesque setting is not going to be the most enjoyable journey I've ever taken. Back on the cart path which winds down off the hill finds you pulling to a stop well to the left of the green as no carts are allowed in that area. Not allowed, but you see guys running right up to the green all the time. Come on, man, a little respect for the course and the rules sure would be nice. Oh, well, what is it they say? "Takes all kinds." Pulling the sand wedge and the putter to save walking back to get that needed club saves time and keeps play moving for the group behind. The walk over to the bunker has me trying to figure out the best shot out of this sand. High bunker wall and ball up close to it means getting it up quickly while still trying to stop it below the pin. Not easy, especially for me. Digging in with an almost sitting position setup, good swing getting a lot of sand finds the ball coming out high for a soft landing. Unfortunately, I land the ball long for about a 15 footer downhill.

Pulling the pin and sizing up the break, I'm thinking. . . . Pull this one off for par and not only would I continue a great round, but this one would put icing on the cake. Ever get nervous in a situation like this? Like life, sometimes we find ourselves in situations that are definitely not earth shattering in terms of their outcome; the anxiety that grabs us, however, is still hard to deal with. I wonder why that is. Right now you would think I was putting for birdie on 18 at Augusta to win the Masters. It is kind of like watching your grandsons play their first basketball or soccer game in Upward. I mean -- and you know what I mean -- you want to get out there and help them do it. They could care less about the outcome. So why are you so anxious that they win? You explain it!

I really like this White Hot #2 center-shafted putter by Odyssey. I re-gripped with the Fatso 5.0 by Super Stroke, and the feel is exactly what I was looking for. The equipment is right if the guy behind the putter can execute. Have you ever seen some guy miss a shot and wrap his club around a tree or throw his stick in a pond? Now how intelligent is that? But it happens and equipment makers just eat it up. That is another one of those "more money than good sense" deals.

Over this putt, rolling it by a little bit is not bad as it would be straight uphill. Just don't leave it short. Never would have guessed, would you? Just one more complete revolution of that little round white ball and it would have been dead center. BOGEY! At least the nerves have vanished.

Still 2 under for the round, can't help feeling that one got away. Why, I don't know. Just thought of something that happened fifty-something years ago. I was fishing with my dad in Canada. Man, what memories! And were those ever great times! My dad had the patience of Job when it came to teaching his two sons how to hunt and fish. On this particularly foggy morning, just me and Dad in the boat (never got any better than that). He was giving all his attention to teaching me the proper technique of how to work a jig. Needless to say, I wasn't catching on and was getting all out of sorts.

Never will forget . . . . Lying there on the boat seat was an old Shakespeare free-spool reel on a steel rod my dad had used forever. And tied on the line was a #6 Eagle Claw hook with just a little bit of nightcrawler on it. Disgusted, I told Daddy I was going to fish with that. "Have at it, son," was his response. Patience galore.

Well, I couldn't cast it with no weight other than that bit of worm, so pulling off a few feet of line, I tossed it over the side of the boat. No sooner did it hit the water than a big smallmouth bass took it. I sat back hard trying to dig the hook in deep, and that dark green colored six-pound plus beauty came out of the water a good three to four feet, dove hard beneath the boat, and came out of the water on the other side of the boat shaking his head trying to throw that hook. Back down and under the boat he went again, this time to run straight into the dip net Dad had stuck down in the water. Almost in one motion Dad had that fish in the net and up in the boat. He reached down to lift that bass out of the net and the hook fell out of its mouth. That beautiful specimen of Canadian aquatic excitement had pulled so hard, all I was doing was holding on. It had straightened out that #6 hook and was just about loose to evade another expectant angular. Had it not been for my dad's quick action, that one too would have gotten away.

Not to be too sentimental, I learned so much from that remarkable man that I think about almost every day. My only regret is that I paid too little attention at times to unquestionable wisdom exuding from a very brilliant man. Miss you, Pap – plan to see you again someday and catch up on some good stuff.

Come to think of it, there are some things in life that we just can't afford to let get away. Set your hook deep into those life-altering experiences and hold on. NET results may be fantastically unimaginable!

CHAPTER **12**

DECEPTIVE

NEMESIS. ACCORDING TO Webster, "an opponent or enemy that is very difficult to defeat." Ever had one? Sure, we all have. And they come in different shapes and sizes, situations, in the games we play and the work we do, and they show up in life all the time. Now some are much more obtrusive than others. But they all show up where they are not welcome or invited. It simply seems to be the nature of the beast.

In the game of golf, our opponent is always the course. We play against the degree of difficulty the course throws at us. Defeat is the name of the game when we face our enemies and in golf, unique in its own disposition, we occasionally get the better of the course but quite often the course seems to deliberately beat us into submission. For some, a score of 90 on a difficult 72 par round would be considered a triumph while for others on that same round, a score of 76 brings about total frustration and disgust having let the course totally destroy them. It makes the game exciting, individualistic, and relative to our own abilities or talent levels. That is exactly why we play. To compete against our "nemesis" when we are playing a game in life can be both strategic and/or plain ole fun.

Realistically, life is not always a fun game and the enemies we do battle with are not always clearly visible and our strategy for competition is not always certain. Let me tell you about a man I will call Ed.

DECEPTIVE

Ed is a great friend, a good Christian man, and a guy who would "give you the shirt off his back." Ed is in a battle; his nemesis. . . cancer. Struggling with this terrible foe for several years now, attacking aggressively his opponent with every means at his disposal has always been his calculated maneuver. Strength and firm faith in the God who sustains him have been his allies.

Unfortunately, just like muscles that atrophy over time due to lack of physical exertion, Ed's eagerness to fight back is waning. Eternity with its assurance of peace and the lack of battles with NO NEMESIS seems to be looming very attractive for him. You know, we simply get tired, don't we? Yet an overwhelming reach is to hold on to every possible moment with the family he loves and has always supported.

Our nemeses often cause a war within that leaves us bewildered due to the direction in which we should plan our next decisive attack. I truly cannot imagine what it would be like to awake from another short, fitful sleep only to realize the battle still rages on. I can only pray for my buddy.

And his beautiful wife of many years, realizing the beginning of another grueling day -- each day in which she is helpless to his defense and totally reliant on others for his care -- how must she feel? Again, so difficult it is for me to consider the possibility of holding my best friend for life realizing that each minute could be the last and contemplating that her strength in that instance would actually be far superior to mine.

Life hurls these types of situations at individuals all the time. There will never be a lapse of these crucial encounters. To be completely upfront, we must prepare ourselves to endure these kinds of battles and aggressively confront this thing called *life* that will assuredly continue to set unforeseen obstacles in our path. God sustains us through life's aggressions. Should it be you don't possess this weapon in your arsenal of defenses, I urgently suggest you fortify your personal armaments by superimposing God's image upon the very mirror of your existence. Eternity will be bliss as a result of engaging in this relationship now.

LIFE IN 18 HOLES

Taking this leisurely ride over to the elevated tee box on #12, I realize I am about to face my nemesis on this course. And sometimes it is true that it is all in your head. But let's face it. Trying so hard to overcome what seems to always be the inevitable is excruciatingly frustrating. Doesn't mean it can never be done, so I just need to "get over it." Completely surrounding any thought of negative outcome to this tee shot with super glue and encasing it to eliminate any secretion of unnerving results is a frantic pursuit that I must immediately engage in. The thought just struck me. . . . I am being confronted with deliberate opportunity to put to sleep any incursion of ballistic intervention in my pursuit of dominance on this hole. With that thought, my attempt to overpower this long par 3 seems extremely unencumbered. Are you kidding me?

This is really a beautiful hole and with proper execution, is one to score well on. From this elevated tee box you look down on an elongated green that leaves plenty of room for error lengthwise but is not very wide. Sand on both sides, especially to the right, but that is not what causes most of the difficulty. Immediately off the tee is a deep gulley completely grown up but in all honesty, of no consequence. Traveling on down the complete length of the left side of the fairway is a sheer embankment, out of bounds on top. And it seems this little parcel of real estate beckons my off the tee with an amazing degree of consistency.

To the right is a hollow totally engulfed in trees and underbrush, and to be expected also is OB. Any tee shot to the right of the sand is going to find itself in this tangled mess and finding the ball is ridiculously insane to attempt. I mentioned the depth of the green. Should the pin placement be forward, I can reach with no more than a 7 iron. However, back placement gives way to a 5 iron. Lots of difference. Wind always seems to be a nuisance and coming straight up out of that hollow or over the hill from the left can create havoc with any well-struck shot. Approaching this shot with the wind actually swirling from seemingly every direction, my focus today is to "minimize my losses."

DECEPTIVE

Pin placement is near center of the green, but anywhere on the putting surface is going to be fantastic today. That will allow for a two-putt which hopefully will allow me to exit this slick-mown, undulating piece of topography unscathed. To stand here with 6 iron in hand relishing what would appear to be the lack of complexity in this shot, two daunting words of the English language come to mind: **deception** and **nemesis.**

Every conceivable encounter of any form of failure to properly execute this shot seems to be flooding my subconscious at this very moment. Drastic measures to denounce any acknowledgement of this propensity to fail must be ingratiated immediately. To put it bluntly, "Get a grip!" Why allow one mentally incapacitated shot negate an otherwise splendid performance of overpowering your enemy, the golf course?

Standing over the shot, everything feels good and unbelievably, a very relaxed nature has taken over. As I made solid contact with the Pro V, it was as though every element of the swing was consciously redeemable. Backswing was smooth with good shoulder turn, shaft was on plane allowing the club head to drive squarely through the ball, and the follow through was as good as I am capable of, ending high and on target.

Holding that position, I watched as my ball launched high and straight with a slight draw which is natural for me. Right at the pin! I could hardly believe my eyes as the ball landed some ten yards beyond the pin and rolled for another fifteen. I thought. . . "Can't hit a 6 iron that far." But I did!

Making my way back to the cart, I couldn't help but recall a prior playing of this hole. My wife was with me. She really enjoys riding in the cart even though she doesn't play. Also, I appreciate the attitude she has about my playing this addictive game as she encourages me to play even more than I do. We always have a great time, just me playing and her criticizing every errant shot that flies off my clubs. As I started down over the steep embankment, the shot off the tee that day with a 5 iron to probably thirty yards straight past the pin was so

LIFE IN 18 HOLES

visible. Then, as I lined up the putt and told Kerry I was going to make it as she doubled over in laughter, we both were aghast as it rolled perfectly into the middle of the cup. Another day. But could it just be possible?

I always find it intriguing how this wonderful thing called a *brain* that we have been blessed with can have such dramatic repercussion when it comes to freezing us in our tracks with disillusionment while on the other hand, can fascinate us with a small morsel of recall that theoretically would only be a blemished identity of history. God has gifted us -- as no other animal -- with the ability to reason and to perpetuate that gifting with unfathomable tendencies of compliance to His desired complexities for the greatest of all creation, the human race.

Oswald Chambers once said: "An elevated mood can only come out of an elevated habit of personal character. If in the externals of your life you live up to the highest you know, God will continually say, 'Friend, go up higher.' " Give that one a thought as the wheels on your cart continue to rotate in this thing called *life*.

Grabbing my putter and racing onto the green, my heart was exploding with excitement. I had pulled the cart to a stop all the way on the backside of the green, and from the first step toward the ball, there was no doubt about the path the ball would take. Have you ever been so sure of something from first glance that you could picture the outcome? That is how it was when I met my wife-to-be. Her beauty and radiance (literally) emphatically destroyed any semblance of creative thinking. And any thought of spending the remainder of my days with any other inferior female was completely vanquished. I was undaunted as to my quest for success in assaulting any obstacle with fury that might possibly stand in my way of a lifelong relationship with this impeccable specimen of opposite sex allurement. Well, whatever it was worked and life is incredibly good. I still love that woman!

Another glance and it was down to pull the pin. Laying it down far out of the way, I took a look back up toward my ball to alleviate any thought of what I had envisioned could even remotely be erroneous. You are not going to believe this. As I gazed up toward the Pro V from the cup, it was like there was a valley meandering its way directly downhill into the center of that little hole in the ground. It was like a stream of water flowing to its destination with ONLY one way to get there.

Back up over the ball, only one obstacle remains. Have to strike the ball hard enough to get it to the sought-after destination, but not so hard that it hits the cup with such velocity that it jumps out. Deep breath and let it out halfway. Kind of like squeezing the trigger on that Remington 270 with the crosshairs firmly fixed on the shoulder of a 6x6 elk in Montana. No jerking the trigger and certainly no miss hits with the putter at this juncture. Straight back and then through the ball, I hear the putter blade make contact with the ball and it is on its way. Gorgeous! I bend low to watch, all the while not hardly believing the finality of what I am about to encounter. There it is again. . . that sound. Nothing like that Pro V pounding into the bottom of the cup. RESOUNDING! Birdie on my **nemesis**! Who was it that wrote that book, *The Power of Positive Thinking*?

Reaching down to retrieve my ball and then replacing the pin, I thought as I fixed my gaze back to that elevated tee box: "I hcpe I live to play you again." Another incredible thought just grabbed me. I am 3 under after 12.

CHAPTER **13**

MY "HOME HOLE" – EVERYBODY NEEDS ONE

HOME HAS ALWAYS been a "needed" place for me. Thinking back over what was probably not a perfect childhood -- although there would not be a whole lot I would change -- I was blessed to grow up with family that loved me and cared about what my future would hold. A lot of money was not always in the back pocket, but we were never hungry or homeless. Bills were never paid late and neighbors were cared about and cared for. Training in practical stuff was important and a good education was encouraged. Common sense was a lifestyle, serving your country was just part of it, and honesty and integrity was a given. Sports? Well, everyone played. Hard work was THE ethic. And God was the Creator and Sustainer. Just no getting around it. Not a bad life, right?

Getting married and having children never interrupted the need for both my wife and me to visit our parents and pay attention to their care. Now, we are the focal point and our children still love coming home. As our family continues to grow, I can only hope that change will nurture that same necessity and desire to keep home the center of everyone's attention.

Meandering around the cart path to #13 tee box, my thoughts are always the same: "Home Hole." To quickly explain, high above and

MY "HOME HOLE" – EVERYBODY NEEDS ONE

looking down on #13 green sits my house. It is always fun to steer the cart alongside the fairway, occasionally seeing Kerry (my wife) out back on the deck cheering me on. When my grandsons are home, they get so excited to see Pap coming. (I always call to let them know.) Not every round will someone be waiting for my appearance. But that does not diminish the fact that the house on the hill is inhabited with a vibrancy and atmosphere that is only recognizable in a place well known as HOME.

Far too often, having spent numerous adult years pastoring a congregation of people, I've witnessed houses inhabited with two or more individuals that are only masquerading the façade of a home. From the outside and to the outside, one would have to think the ideal family coexists within the framework of a very congenial and loving relationship. Too many gaps often exist that are allowed to go or uncared for or attended to with the end result being the dismantling of the structure that has long been the cornerstone of our American society, the traditional family. Those gaps may result from seeking so-called happiness through artificial means such as alcohol or drugs; failure to nurture spousal needs leading to outside-the-marriage relationships that destroy the very fabric of the institution; failure to discipline and provide structure for children who are crying out for allegiance from unreciprocating parents; and countless other enigmas that are fracturing the very bones of the skeleton of the family. With the decadence of the family structure, we should not be surprised that our prisons are full, young people are ill-nourished to compete in the workplace, and cohabiting rather than tying a solid knot is the acceptable alternative. Recall this. "Around and around it goes and where it stops nobody knows." So, okay. It's time to tee it up on 13 – there's another group not far behind.

Thirteen is a par 5 -- actually fairly easy par 5 -- that doglegs slightly to the left to a huge green that has all kinds of movement on it. From the blue tees you hit directly over a hollow ("holler" in KY) that is a proverbial thicket to the left. Just stay away from it and that is not hard to do. A couple of bunkers loom to right of the fairway and they do have a tendency to get in the way. A good strong tee shot beyond the last bunker will find you in the upper middle of the short grass and a phenomenal run over the hill is possible. Having said that, come up short and you have a heck of a long way to go.

Wherever you are for that second stroke, it is all downhill with a decently wide fairway to that beautiful, undulating green that simply stands up pretty high above where the short grass ends. Large bunkers protect the center of the green and also skirt the upper right side. Hit it too far. . . well, there is a pond back there. It seems most golfers shy away from the bottom or left side of the green as it drops off pretty drastically. Result? Lot of balls in those bunkers to the right which leaves you trying to get out of the sand to a lot of downhill slope which many times is not the greatest of places to be.

Talking about that lower side of the green. . . . If you have enough guts to hit it down that way and come up a little short, you are always chipping uphill and it is very easy to stop the ball right where you want it. Yep! Win some – lose some. But this is just a gorgeous setting for a well defined par 5 that gives up several birdies. Not overly aggressive yet calculating, and you can walk away to the short par 3 having scored very well.

Teeing my Pro V low, I want to keep the ball down to penetrate a stiff breeze that is directly in my face. For some reason, confidence off this tee is never a problem for me and today seems to be no different as I approach this setup, expecting better than average results. Most any analytical thinker will tell you that confidence is always a contributing factor in solving both complex and uncomplicated problems. However, in the society we find ourselves inhabiting today, lacking in this most crucial commodity seems to broadcast despondency and lurks as a depraving factor in the molecular makeup of many individuals. Yes, I do believe it can be genetic! Have you ever heard the phrase, "Poverty breeds poverty"? So many times we encounter individuals totally diminished to a subservient culture with no urgency to rise above the quagmire of the status quo that has relinquished itself to the despotism of following its hierarchy, regardless

MY "HOME HOLE" – EVERYBODY NEEDS ONE

of how unemancipated that individual is from the clutches of another. Confidence is something we cannot necessarily teach, but it *can* exude through proper training, education, and association with those people who seem to be "eaten up with it" (pardon the phrase). Breaking away from where you have always been may seem deviant rather than normal. But really, who wants to just be NORMAL? Go for it! I heard John Calipari, coach of the Kentucky Wildcats basketball team, talking about his players. He wants them to "succeed and proceed." Not a bad thought, you think?

Aiming point -- everybody needs one -- is the far side of that last bunker I mentioned. Just beyond that point and you will get a bunch of roll down the fairway. By the way, thinking about life. . . . What are you aiming for? Many of us have "been there and done that", so to speak, but we never have the option of calling it quits, sneaking back into a hole somewhere, and waiting out our time. If you have already helped yourself enough and secured your future, try being a mentor to someone who is working toward the same target you shot at and hit, or to the one determined but struggling to get over the hump. Bible says that wisdom retained rather than shared is actually pathetic and has no residual value.

For all of you, youth as your ally or older age a waterfall you are swimming upstream from in order not to be overtaken by its current, perhaps you too are standing on the 13th tee. But it is life that is staring you in the face rather than a fairway. My advice is that you aim for the far side of that last bunker, make preparation for a lot of roll even though there may be a lot of bumps down the way, and plan your approach that may just leave you lying two on the putting surface of the par 5 of life. Who knows? Maybe eagle or birdie!

Or perhaps a few of those unthinking, unappreciative souls you are following have left a lot of divots that seem to all be right in your way. So you three-putt. But take notice. That is still par and when we shoot par in this thing called *life*, we have played the course straight up. Concentrate, focus, and eliminate the bogey. Never settle for less.

Great contact – the ball seemed to explode off the face of my 10.5

degree driver. Piercing through the wind with a low trajectory, the ball makes contact with the ground at what could not have been a better place and quickly is out of sight down the fairway that slopes away from me. Confidence? We talked about it. Couldn't be any higher as I slip the head cover back on my driver. Sliding under the wheel of perpetual motion, the golf cart, thoughts of a somewhat level lie and reachable in two are predominate. Negotiating the steep downhill path and the laborious climb up the other side, I get my first glimpse of what awaits – SWEET! Hey, man, this was kind of like the first time I saw my wife. Couldn't wait to get close and figure out what my next move would be. Pulling to a stop, I could hardly believe how well the ball was sitting up. This is usually a good hole for me, but rarely is there off the tee results that render such extraordinary opportunity to reach this slightly elevated green in two.

How many times does life offer up such tremendous potential for success that we can do nothing less than go all out and see what happens? Now I know real life decisions are more critical than my decision on this next shot, but sometimes circumstances warrant throwing it all in and going for broke. Sink or swim, there is just no way of getting around pulling the trigger. I know. Sometimes it almost makes us sick to think "what if" even when we know opportunity of such magnitude seldom comes. But think. . . . The heavyweight contender knows he didn't win the crown in that 15-round bout. It was all the hard training that propelled him over the top to victory. If you have done your homework, put in the grueling work of preparation and calculation, sacrificed and determined to perpetuate winning in your life, then pull out the big stick and go for it! My thought: If you have truly run the gauntlet leading up to such a once-in-a-lifetime happening, you probably have a little reserve in the tank to get you to the next one even if things don't work out as anticipated. Be strong, braveheart!

Did I mention a great lie? And only 165 out. Downhill but the green does set up so, this is a difficult one for me to figure out. There is no way I am not going for it. I carry two hybrids in my bag – a 4

MY "HOME HOLE" – EVERYBODY NEEDS ONE

and 5 Adams V4. These clubs are incredibly easy to hit, and knowing the distance I usually get makes pulling the 5 hybrid seem like a little much. Factoring in the wind and realizing I'll have to get the ball up quickly and maintain good elevation on the shot, the 6 iron is not going to be enough club. Pulling the head cover from the 5 and stepping behind the ball to visually determine the best approach, I notice my breath coming a bit quickly as the adrenalin kicks in. This is really exciting and something (just "gut", I guess) tells me I am going to pull this one off.

Head down, concentrating on the ball. . . the sound that penetrated my eardrums was beautiful and I didn't even have to look up to know that ball was struck well. Continuing the follow through automatically allows me to visually locate the path of the Pro V and the little draw that was curling the ball toward the upper side of the green. The distance was perfect and it settled down with some roll to the left and downhill that actually leaves me putting across the green rather than down over the slope that is always unpredictable. Couldn't help but look up and say, "Thank you, Jesus", even knowing He is probably not too interested in my golf game.

Or is He? I serve a big God who is totally engrossed in big things for us, but I also think He smiles sometimes when we accomplish something that is absolutely less than important. And probably laughs out loud when thinking we had the audacity to believe we had pulled off something of significance. After all, He told us to talk to Him about everything, never fail to ask for anything when we are in His will . . . but I still don't know if that includes my golf game. Anyway, take that shot any day!

I told you about the over-sized grip on my putter. Well, I can't wait to see how good it will feel standing over a putt for EAGLE. Back in the cart and racing down the cart path, I catch a glimpse of #14 tee box. I almost shudder with intense exuberance reflecting upon several months ago when Caleb (my son) and I were playing that short par 3. But that's another story and you will definitely hear about it. Seldom does an opportunity such as this present itself and especially

LIFE IN 18 HOLES

now, as I glance up the hill to the back of my house hoping that Kerry is watching. She's not! Still – this is "Home Hole." Doesn't get any better.

In this game called *golf* that many of us mutilate yet we play on, eagle is an outstanding accomplishment. As opposed to par, two under is rather significant and certainly is not an everyday event even for those who earn their living on the tour. To compete at that level consistently, so much better than average, turns heads and in many cases launches the competitor to record achievement which often brings great reward. In his book *7 MEN*, author Eric Metaxas outlines the heroics of seven men with various endeavors from athlete to politician to religious leader who overcame severe challenges only to blossom to greatness in their respective pursuits. If you haven't read this book – get it! Now these men, with the exception of one, were not playing games. Yet the level of excellence they walked in should provide impetus for all of us regardless of our life's execution. So if we are only playing for fun with no real consequence to the outcome or competing for prominence in what could be a global game changer, performing to the degree of "eagle" excellence is a formidable challenge we should all wrap our arms around.

This thing is almost totally straight, falling off just maybe half a cup right at the hole. Putting uphill ever so slightly on this beautiful piece of real estate that should really hold its line, speed is critical and it must be struck solidly. On its way and right on line, but momentum dwindles and my Pro V comes to a stop one turn short of dropping into the hole. Hey, the result may not have a lasting impact on anything, but I really wanted that one! That's why we compete -- at anything!

Wait a minute. I am four under and I can't wait to let you in on what's coming next. LIFE! Ain't it good?

CHAPTER **14**

HOLE-IN-ONE

THAT OVERSIZE PUTTER grip. . . . Well, it did feel pretty good taking on that putt for eagle. Reality though once again takes its toll as I slide under the wheel thinking about who all I would have called **IF** I had made that one for eagle. Climbing the long, winding uphill path to "Tom Foolery", the name given to hole # 14 (all the holes on this course have been given unique names), I wonder who was the initiator of this less-than-glamorous name for this short par 3. But just like so many other things, I doubt it really matters.

About something that does matter and before we tee it up, I want to direct a question to all you guys and gals that hold dear your beloved game of golf and who have fathered or mothered children. A very culinary (if you will) question, knowing you will salivate over the complexity and enormity of your answer. The absolute beauty of this question lies in the fact that it is different for all of us, holds more grandeur for some than others, and is unlimited in its capacity to exist. The sheer spiking of some of your remembrances will be electrifying to say the least, while for others a more somber atmosphere will permeate your innermost and perhaps seclusive reactions. The reason for such exorbitant differences is perhaps a result of unbelievable conquests, the very framework of family nomenclature, regrettable and irretrievable loss, or the mere proclivity toward a docile existence. Nonetheless, the question holds unfathomable merit and is deserving of intense scrutiny. I certainly intend it not to be provocative but rather to arouse acute awareness and aggression toward the rationale of this thing called *life*.

Posing this question is somewhat awkward. However, here is my feeble attempt. Drawing from the myriad of life experiences, from which of the following categories come the most compellingly memorable or perhaps even life-altering occurrences? Interaction with and love of family? Vocation successes or failures? Or friendships? I choose to limit your selection to one of only three, even though I personally believe there is another choice that has dramatically positioned me in this life to look forward to a glorious life throughout all eternity. My greatest accomplishment in life was recognizing Jesus Christ as my personal Savior and that has been a life changer for me. Understandably, not all of you reading these pages have experienced this same blessing. I can only pray that you will, and respect and love you for who you are. Still friends?

For me, work has always been fun. Friends have always been sought for and sought out. But family has always provided me with my most formidable challenges, opportunities for perpetual happiness, and my most memorable experiences. One of those crescendo moments took place right here on the short par 3, hole # 14, named "Tom Foolery" by someone, from the white tees. And I will never forget it.

It all took place on May 17, 2013. But before I indulge in the fineries of an unforgettable experience, allow me to retreat to the field of eligible participants to whom the question was posed: parents and golfers, the core of which I fit both. Parenting has been a phenomenal experience for my wife and me. I know. Nothing new. Right? And this certainly does not throw us into the category of exception. However, we do have exceptional children. Our two, self-driven not parent-driven, pursued academic excellence with a fervor. Each of them deliberately, emphatically, and recklessly walked away from the personal applause of popularity to pursue and compete in the academic arena. That is not to say they were hideaways, non-receptive to

HOLE-IN-ONE

the cultural equivalencies around them. They were merely searching for and envisioning deeper reality and accomplishment of future endeavors that would far out-distance the "cool" of the moment.

A solid belief system encrusted their very being and they have both pursued a relationship with their Creator, Redeemer, and best Friend. Philosophically, they have driven down somewhat different paths, all the time maintaining a beautiful relationship with one another. Our daughter and her husband have dramatically enhanced our lives with three gregarious little boys while my son and his beautiful wife are still working out the details.

Kerry and I have experienced times of exponential elation stemming from the antics of our children, and we have also been driven to our knees when life-in-the-balance issues were threatening. Such things are what peered into my intellect and with intensity challenged this query to only this elite group, moms and dads who are golfers. My hope is that you will embellish this question to the point of lucrative self-disposition.

Allow me once again to recall. It was May 17th, 2013. My son Caleb and I were competing aggressively for top honors, with his dear old dad actually getting the better of him. All that changed in dramatic fashion with one swing of his TaylorMade 54 degree wedge, which by the way I gave him.

On that fateful day, ball teed up near middle of the white markers, my son stared down over his Slazenger ball. My memory tells me it was a gorgeous day and that swing. . . well, it was just as beautiful. Cabe has a long turn on his backswing, strikes the ball with an enormous amount of clubhead speed, and his follow through is quite good. His line of sight was taking him from ball to the flagstick, which was tucked down in a little pocket near the front of the green only 109 yards away. I watched as the ball lifted off that grassy tee box (result of a perfect ball strike), gaining extraordinary height. I distinctly remember saying, "It's right at it!" And thinking, "Be good! Be good!"

Special moments provoking ballistic memories, the kind that never cease to increase in intensity, to me are superimposed when a member of my family ignites the circumstance. Let me give you a "for instance". My dad and his two little boys (I was barely five at the time and Jack was six.) were walking up Shaddamaw Branch just off Elk Lick Holler watching Queenie, a little Feist hunting dog, work a hillside to our left. It was squirrel season and all of a sudden she barks *treed*. Schucks! She was halfway up the side of that steep hill and neither Jack nor myself was big enough to climb it.

So being the dad that Dad was, he picked us both up, handed Ralph his buddy who was with us the little single shot .22 caliber rifle, and carried us up the hill. Dad or Ralph one spotted the squirrel curled around a limb looking at us. Took Dad forever to point that thing out to us. But finally -- and since Jack was the oldest -- it was his shot first. Firstborn man thing, I guess. That's okay. I want you to know, he pulled the trigger, and out rolled that little critter. He had shot its eyes out! Not bad for a six- year-old.

Dad turned and looked at me. "Your turn," he said. I didn't have a clue as to what was going on, but there was another squirrel up that same tree. After considerable urging from Dad and Ralph, I was holding that .22 square on my first squirrel and squeezing the trigger. Rest is history. To you that may not sound exciting, memorable, or even worth talking about. But for me, that particular moment will always be a highlight of my life. And my DAD, a man I miss dearly, was the instigator.

Watching intently the flight of Cabe's ball, it seemed to take forever before it landed some 112 yards from the tee. You may recall the pin was at 109 yards, rangefinder yardages. Coming down just to the left of the cup and beyond it, the spin he had on the ball kicked in. Amazingly and shockingly, we watched the ball trickle ever so slowly back down the incline and drop into the middle of the cup. I wish I could tell you our reaction as we looked at each other. It seemed it was almost subdued – for an instant! I will never forget the look on his face, captured on my iPhone, as he retrieved the ball from the cup. I can only imagine how *my* dad felt as he carried me and my brother back down off that hill! Moms and dads, things like that are what

HOLE-IN-ONE

initiated the profundity of my question.

What is it they say? "Today is a different day." Sitting in the cart next to the blue tees, I fix my gaze on the flag. Pin position today is far back right corner making this a fairly long par 3. Going right at the pin would mean crossing two bunkers that guard the front right of the green and neither are a piece of cake to get out of. To be real honest, my best offense on this hole today is to play middle of green and plan on a two-putt to walk away safe.

Wind being somewhat of a problem, I want to club up enough to reach back middle of green. Pulling 8 iron, plenty of club to execute the plan, I search out a nice level spot near the right marker to tee up my ball, trying to use all available real estate to the left. Success today would mean walking off with par and concentrating on attack mode on #15.

All good tacticians, although confident of their well-thought-out plan, always have a Plan B. You see, even the greatest tactical maneuver may encounter a glitch, so something to fall back on is always strategically practical. The problem with this great game called *golf*? Plan B probably means you just cost yourself a stroke. My glitch off the tee was a very poor stroke resulting in a push to the right which resulted in not enough distance which resulted in a plugged ball in the face of the second bunker to the right. A super thought just legitimized itself in my cranial equilibrium. . . . What a great time for a mulligan! Problem. I don't have a mulligan. Know what? Looks like potential is probable for a dropped shot on this once so thrilling par 3.

Have you ever been in a situation where you simply did what you had to do and hoped for the best? Life throws those kinds of curves at us occasionally. I have more than likely said it before, but when faced with the possibility of striking out, use every resource available to minimize your losses. There will usually be another day with another incredible opportunity to crawl out of the last hole you so brilliantly dug for yourself. Think about it. . . . That's what makes life so intriguing!

◄ **LIFE IN 18 HOLES**

Digging solidly into the sand, my only option is to hit it hard and hope for the best -- the best being getting out of this bunker. Well, I'm out! But I've flown the green leaving myself with a difficult pitch shot back toward a hole running away from me. Now bogey is my goal and par is only a distant memory. Thankfully, the pitch and run worked quite well and the four-foot putt dropped for only one over. Looking back, this could have really been disastrous.

Times like these make for an awfully long walk back to the cart. Halfway back across the green, I can't refuse a glimpse down toward the front edge of the putting surface. There, stoically positioned is that little pocket which once so unforgettably housed the pin position that my son stared down for a hole-in-one. Phenomenal memory! And this time MY BOY was the instigator!

CHAPTER **15**

GETS ME EVERY TIME

HAVE YOU EVER entered into an agreement, made an offer to purchase, or struck a deal of some sort knowing that your calculated maneuver could prove to be flawed in its outcome? Even when we have been burned before, it seems human diagnostics are recurringly faulty when tallied against a particular event in which we are determined to succeed. Our drive -- or should I say our DESIRE -- is so overwhelmingly addictive that all rational behavior is circumvented.

So it is for me going off #15 tee. I am so bereft of logical exposure on this hole that it is insanely amazing. Insane in that every time I step between the tee markers, my gaze is what I think is straight down the middle but emphatically I know better. You see, what seems to be middle of the fairway is actually to the right (if that makes any sense), and it seems my natural inclination is to fade the ball on this hole. You are exactly right. A fade here means losing it to the right and more than likely out of bounds. Or at least a second shot in which the green is totally obliterated from sight. My failure to defy my weakness often proves fatal to what could be or <u>should</u> be a reasonably good scoring hole. In other words, the way this hole sets up for me does not bode well in propelling myself to a low score on the back nine.

However, when mind does not succumb to matter and my cravings for ball flight down the right side of the fairway are overcome, results can prove to be most rewarding. As a matter of fact, flying the top of the hill that turns to a slight dogleg right means a bunch of roll over a steep incline, thus adding a lot of yards to the tee shot. Hit perfectly with the added value of the roll and a second shot of just over 100 yards is definitely doable and usually straight at the pin. There again. . . perfect for me is an eloquent over-exaggeration of the art of ball striking on my part, and less- than-sought-after results are more prevalent and painful. But who knows? Stranger things have happened!

Mentioned earlier, every hole on this course has its own distinct name. Number 15 is simply called "Sycamore", deriving its name, I assume, from a huge sycamore tree shading the green to the front and left. *Platanus occidentalis,* its scientific name (also called a *buttonwood*), this tree grows to be 100 feet tall and sometimes larger. It produces a dense green foliage and is perfect for shade. The sycamore is one of the oldest species of trees on the earth and is known for its longevity and hardiness. The enormous leaves turn yellow in the fall, making for a beautiful touch of color at the end of growing season. The white trunk wrapped about by a segmented and curling greenish-gray bark makes this tree beautiful to the sight and a favorite of many.

The large and long limbs of the sycamore appear very stately; however, they can be very obtrusive to the golfer. A tremendous tee shot off #15 can set up a disastrous second into the green, albeit the ancient sycamore that guards the front entrance with ferocious intimidation. Now I am not saying the tree is right in your way. . . hardly. But I have seen it jump out and trounce upon the most well-intentioned second shot, dropping it down into the thick rough or seemingly obliterating its existence from the face of the earth never to be seen again. By the way, that will cost you a stroke. A lot of guys don't like this tree!

And why is it that some folks want to build houses right on the fairway? Well, I really do know the answer to that question, but it doesn't make you feel any better when your errant tee shot makes contact with that piece of architectural integrity otherwise known as an inhabited structure or *home*. Just another undocumented reason for going right off the tee to avoid broken glass. Homeowners on golf courses, although expectantly undefendable, are not overzealous at adding to their collection of golf balls in the family room.

Oh! I forgot to mention. . . there **is** a water hazard some 25 yards in front of the green and bunkers to the right. But if you totally dismiss the negative appeal to #15 and play it for what it is, you will be infatuated with the challenge and the serene beauty of this meticulously laid-out marvel. The course architect had a lot to work with when legitimizing "Sycamore" and did bountiful work while creating the atmosphere surrounding this hole. Well done, my friend!

Have you ever heard the old adage, "Timing is everything"? This is often attributed to successful business endeavors, particular plays in sporting events, or it could even have been very logistical in the eventual capturing of your beloved soulmate. But far beyond hypotheticals, the well-sculptured #15 green on Old Silo epitomizes the essence of timing for a playing partner we will call Rick.

Our foursome, due to tightly booked tee times, was asked to tee off from the back side, and had only banged out five holes when evident irregularities overcame our buddy Rick, and he passed out in the middle of the green. He hadn't been feeling good and was prescribed some strong medication. Quickly to his feet, he attributed this unforeseen development to what he was taking. However, in a matter of less than a minute, Rick was on the ground two more times, and it was very apparent to the three of us that this situation was far more complicated than first anticipated. With Rick in the cart, a call goes out on that miraculous piece of logic defilement called a cell phone, and medical attention would meet us at the clubhouse. We weren't aware at the time, but timing may have been in his behalf.

To make a long story short, emergency room doctors determined that Rick's blood sugar levels were in the plus 400's . . . dangerously high! Since that time, measures have been taken to bring under control a medical problem that he didn't even realize was an issue for him. I believe "timing" could have been everything for Rick.

You know (not saying this was the case with my playing partner), sometimes we ignore or postpone definition of obvious abnormalities that could be very detrimental to our health. Is it worth it? Maybe you are all right with disavowing the obvious, but at least be cognizant of how it may affect your family. I know the spiritual guru Job declared in 14:1, "Man that is born of a woman is of few days and full of trouble." But why expound upon the problem by dismissing telltale signs of danger and exaggerate the calamity that could await the ones you love most? Remember, they too have a staggering investment in what you epitomize to be your own – your life! When I put title to this chapter, believe me, I was not referring to a heart attack.

Standing between the blue tee markers, I have just made a deliberate decision; however, I have yet to see whether it will prove rewarding. Deliberate decisions are what I consider to be time-consuming intercessories based on desired eventualities. Have you ever really put in the time and mental exhaustion to arrive at a truly deliberate decision? Hey, I am not kidding!

In all honesty I am afraid that not too many people do. When you observe their lives -- their habits, their indulgences, their inconsistencies -- you don't have to be a fruit inspector to calculate the illegitimate process of their decision-making. Please. Refrain now from awaking one day in the future only to realize that wanton disregard for things necessary and desperately needed has proliferated your life. Get a grip! This thing called *life* with all its mesmerizing accessories is the **most** important adult game you will ever play.

That decision . . . it's 3 wood instead of driver off the tee today. This is a good club for me and my confidence skyrockets when I pull it from the bag. Remember I mentioned those homes to the left? Well, they are practically lining the cart path. However, an excellent aiming point is a fairway bunker just right of the cart path nestled into the left side of the fairway just before dropping over the steep dogleg right. There is an excellent landing area but the tee shot must be pretty well positioned. Actually, this spot affords the golfer the only true flat lie for a second into the green.

Stiff wind blowing straight at me. If I can keep the ball flight low, the possibility of the wind knocking it down a bit is okay. Might come up a little short, but should be able to handle my approach distance into the green with not much difficulty. Great contact! Ball flight is right on line, fading just a little, and surprisingly, I'm getting a good roll. Going to like this next shot!

Beautiful ball position and an absolutely gorgeous view down at the green! There is even a glimpse from here of the course namesake, "The Old Silo". Even though the huge sycamore looms large from this angle, a well-shaped shot starting right at that tree and fading ever so slightly is a perfect setup. That strong wind and distance out make for ideal conditions and opportunity to pull another high-confidence club, the V4 #5 Hybrid by Adams. Gazing down at that beautiful putting surface, my commitment to this shot is absolute and now all I have to do is pull it off.

Again, solid contact! Man, there is just something unexplainable about the feel of a well-struck shot. Fascinated, I watch the ball curl into the green with just the right amount of fade and settle in about fifteen feet directly below the pin. I hope no one is watching as I hold the club in the follow-through position for what seems forever, simply glowing at the results. Listen. This doesn't happen to me that often. That was a perfect shot in anyone's book.

You know, considering life, it is so exhilarating to think that I have been placed directly in the middle of creation and have been afforded the opportunity to take full advantage of all its benefits. This is phenomenal! And never should there be the audacity to take such wonderful exposure for granted. I read constantly about folks who really believe that just by virtue of being placed on God's green earth they are entitled to certain amenities. The people of this "greatest of all" countries seem to have taken on an entitlement nature and their expectations are through the roof. ENTITLED! Life was given; choices avail themselves; and **stuff** is earned! My thoughts . . . for all you seekers of a free ride. I'll be like Shaq in that Gold Bond commercial: "Man up!" Well, I assume it's time to dispense with this philosophical diatribe – I have a putt to make!

◄ LIFE IN 18 HOLES

Cart path is steep on this downhill descent. Letting the cart hold itself back, I simply enjoy the view while dropping off the hill. Grabbing the Odyssey with the Fatso 5.0 Super Stroke grip, it's time to get mentally ready to make this putt for birdie. Golf certainly is a mental game, and putting seems to push all limits of cranial capacity. Reading the green can reveal an obvious line at times, while at others, determining the direction of the break seems practically impossible.

Speed is another thing altogether. Ideally, your aiming point is approximately a foot beyond the hole, but it sure does seem awfully easy to leave it short or run it by a bunch. This thing called *putting* can be extremely frustrating if you don't have your head on right. All things taken into account, I have never seen anyone "make them all."

Observing every angle of this putt, this thing is nothing but dead straight and uphill. Getting the speed right is critical, but I know it will take a pretty fair rap to get it to the cup. As I take the ball mark away and deposit it in my pocket, I feel good about the expected results. Couple of practice swings from behind the ball, all the while zoned in on the line, I step into position totally committed to the line. Smooth takeaway and follow through and the Pro V is on its way.

I am playing the new high number Pro V's my son got me. I really do enjoy hitting these bad boys. In this cooler weather, like any other ball, the tendency is for a little less distance. But in the dead of summer -- high temps -- these things jump off the club with distance and ball flight that is incredible. Trouble is, I don't play these too often because I can't afford to. Too expensive for my blood. When these are gone, I will just have to wait for Caleb to come through again.

It doesn't take very long to roll that perfectly round ball fifteen feet. However, when it starts slowing down short of the cup, it seems like an eternity. Now why did I do that? It is uphill all the way, no reason to not have enough speed, and watch it pull up one. . . one turn short. Man, that is crazy! A tap-in par. Have you ever stopped, scratched your head, and thought, "What could have been"? That's life. And that's golf!

CHAPTER **16**

SIGNATURE HOLE

DELIVERED A COUPLE of days ago via USPS -- the latest edition of *Traveler,* the official magazine of Hilton Grand Vacation Club. Granted, these featured locations are seldom or remotely ever a destination adventure. But it never hurts to look. It is kind of like in the several years past, the Sears & Roebuck catalogue. Country folks used to call it the "Wish Book".

So let me tell you what was on the cover . . . "DOWN UNDER"! You know where that is. I have always wanted to go to Australia. Came close one time while in the military, but things didn't go as planned. Oh, well.

Several PGA professionals hail from that brilliant land of contrasts. Adam Scott, Masters champion and seemingly all-around good guy, cut his teeth learning the game of golf there and learn he did. Perfect swing mechanics – really enjoy watching him play.

On many of the different courses in Australia, commentators speak of that "signature hole". These are those ideal layouts, usually beautiful, and known for one distinct or unique feature that sets that one hole apart from all the others. We too have a "signature hole" on this renowned 18- hole course.

As you jump back in the cart after finishing up on #15, cross the creek and twist around to #16 tee box, there it is. Namesake for the course. "The Old Silo". . . brilliantly festooning the left side of the fairway some 300 yards out from the blue tees. This is not the first time you will have seen this crafted masterpiece. Actually, on #6 you get your first glimpse and for that reason, the hole is aptly named. This time however, you get to play right alongside it. I mentioned a long time ago that the course was carved out of a large farm here in Montgomery County. Namesake of the course, the silo was once used for storing grain or *silage*, as it is called, that was harvested from the farm. This cut-stone structure was meticulously crafted. Its sturdiness is still apparent upon examination and definitely could be used again, although that probably will never be reality. Its usefulness has come and gone, but its aesthetic value makes viewing this historical landmark for the first time crushingly inspiring. Evidently, Graham Marsh, former PGA player and first owner/developer of the course, was more than impressed.

Number 16 plays some 400 yards from the blue tees and over 430 from the tips. A good, wide fairway plays right alongside the silo and if you do push your tee shot or succumb to that dreaded severe slice (for the right hander), you get relief as #6 fairway runs parallel for a good distance with this one. There are some major bunkers right between the two fairways, and you really need to stay out of those well-placed obstructions. The cart path curls around squarely in front of the green at the far end of the fairway with a creek ("water hazard", they call it) looming large just beyond where the carts run.

Good scores are not uncommon, but there is one recipe for success on #16 that definitely cannot be ignored: DISCIPLINE! Speaking of . . . . My wife and I were playing another course not long ago (she actually doesn't play, but really enjoys the ride) when she was the first to pick up on what we consider to be a major infraction. Maybe that is not the best way to describe what we observed, but nonetheless the event that unfolded involving the foursome in front of us was disgustingly discouraging for several reasons.

I had spoken to that group not long before. It appeared to be a grandfather, father, and two young -- but grown in body -- sons. First reason: One of the boys attempted a chip shot just off the green and muffed it, just barely carrying onto the fringe. Unable to control himself (in other words, his temper got the best of him), he gave his club a sling in the direction of the cart, and turns out it was right on target. Bouncing off the cart, hopefully with no damage to either, it was good that no one was standing close. To complicate matters, he jerked the flagstick out of the cup and slammed it down, leaving a good gouge in the putting surface that was left unrepaired. Secondly, and what I consider to be an even greater malady, neither the dad nor granddad addressed the issue with the young man, missing a very teachable moment. Granted, the discipline mentioned that's needed to play #16 is a far cry removed from the LACK OF DISCIPLINE --same word denoting extraordinary differences -- displayed in the aforementioned exploit.

Call it what you want, but far too many young people get into far too much trouble directly attributed to LACK OF DISCIPLINE. Disrespect of other people's properties (in this case the cart and the putting surface, actually only rented and certainly not owned) is a major problem. That disrespect, I believe, stems directly from the discipline issue which in so many cases goes completely unaltered in great part due to the LACK OF DISCIPLINE exemplified from the perceived authority figure. In this case, the dad and granddad. I say *granddad* because I believe I would do my grandsons a grave injustice should I allow similar situations to go unaddressed or dealt with. The blame attributed to the son for his antics is certainly justifiable; however, greater blame, as well as shame, needs to be pinned on the parent for allowing such outlandish action on the part of his son.

Come on, moms and dads. Honestly, I think most of you agree with me. We do our most precious commodities no favors by defending them when they are wrong or failing to discipline when circumstances warrant our aggressive action. I realize it is a tough world that our children are growing up in. Show them wisdom and not ignorance. They will respect you immensely. "Spare the rod and spoil the child." I read that in a best seller and I believe you know the one I am referring to. Harsh? Really!

LIFE IN 18 HOLES

Did I mention *discipline* when playing #16? This is that other *discipline* I was referring to when it takes every morsel of tenacity you can muster to lay up and not go for it in two. Let's say your tee shot was less than brilliant, you are a long way out and maybe can't even see the pin, you know the creek is there, but you really want to reach the green in two. Yep, this is an easy scoring hole . . . if you had a good tee shot. But what about the water? I can't count on hands and toes the times I have seen guys really get aggressive, only to find their next shot coming up wet and there went the good score. Probably double! Hindsight says, "Lay up and play an easy sand wedge close and walk away with a par." On the other hand, there is just something intriguing about going for it, right? So we fail to execute. It is only a game! My dad always said, "Show me a man who never failed and I will show you a man who never tried anything."

Teeing up to the right side of the box, I want to use all the available fairway I have to the left. Left side just beyond the 150-marker in the shadow of "Old Silo", itself is perfect. As I watch intently, my ball lands pretty much where I wanted it, kicks right just a little, and gets a fairly good roll. Don't you enjoy pulling something off almost exactly as planned? Not only is it good for the confidence, but sometimes it feels quite good to gloat a little bit (only on the inside of course).

Rolling to a stop beside my ball, I can't help but admire the signature piece that highlights this course. Just sitting for a moment to look, I am enthralled thinking of all the hard work that went into putting that monument together. An awful lot of sweat -- and perhaps some blood and tears -- culminated in a workable masterpiece that served the farm owner well. Filled to the top meant his cattle would fare pretty well during those cold winter months, resulting in a spring market that would fill his pocketbook and allow him to do it all again. Farming is hard work. Another saying my dad had that will always be borne out: "Hard work never hurt nobody." Pap never had much empathy for laziness! Flag is dead in the middle today. Rangefinder verifies that 8 iron is perfect and I should be able to leave it just a little short with a perfect uphill putt. Would you believe it? I just had

SIGNATURE HOLE

another confidence-building, pulled- it-off shot again that I spoke of earlier. This gloating thing could become habit forming.

The little bridge over the creek awaits my appearance as I slide back onto the seat of the cart. The water on this hole always looks fantastic when you are safely on the other side. Walking across what almost seems like a mini swinging bridge, one can't help but notice those round white objects staring up from the water. They should have laid up, but there just was not the discipline. Unfortunately, they went for it.

Did I ever tell you that one of the most thrilling audible experiences anyone can have is when that little engineering marvel called a *golf ball* finds its way to the bottom of that moulded round piece of plastic called a *cup*? From eight feet away I was just entertained by the melody that reverberated out of that little hole in the ground. Ain't it good? I will walk off this luscious piece of real estate with another birdie. I would say that this is like heaven on earth, but that best seller again . . . . "Eye has not seen, ear has not heard, nor has it entered into the heart of man. . . ." I really can't even imagine the bliss that will unfold within those portals of glory, so how can I compare?

You know, I firmly believe there are still a bunch of fantastic opportunities that await me as I trudge through this thing called *life*. I certainly don't know what I will encounter or even the possible difficulty that I may have to face. As good as it is here, I can hardly wait for what is being fashioned for me after I putt out and walk off that final green in this life. I get excited when I think of the words of Jesus: "I go to prepare a place for you . . . ."

CHAPTER **17**

EASY PEASY

HAVE I MENTIONED the movie *The Greatest Game Ever Played*? Pretty sure I did. Anyway, if you are a golfer and haven't, you need to see this movie. Briefly. . . Francis Quimet, a rookie, plays in the U.S. Open and defeats Harry Vardin, who some say was the greatest player of all time. Not giving away much more of this legendary film, Eddie is probably my favorite character. Eddie is a little, short, roly-poly young boy who (under too-long-to-mention circumstances) becomes the caddy for Francis.

This little guy Eddie is hilarious and comes up with some of the greatest sayings imaginable. One is, "Read it, roll it, hole it!" Another -- consequently the reasoning behind the title of this chapter and following on the heels of a terrific putt made by Francis -- "Easy peasy lemon squeezy!" His mannerisms and expressions are exceptional and actually, a little over the top at times. But without Eddie, the movie would be less than appealing to say the least.

So why did Eddie's expression of characterizing that putt come to mind when titling this chapter? Hole #17 is really that easy! A short par 4 probably reachable for the really long hitters. All you have to do is keep it left off the tee and the rest is history -- par history at least. And birdies even come pretty often.

However, *easy* does not mean there is no danger lurking if concentration is lost. Have you ever noticed that accomplishments of any nature can be railroaded if we take a whimsical approach to our effort? In other words, any task worth succeeding at must be cautiously and methodically advanced with seriousness and accountability. Even a golf shot. So many times we are guilty of allowing repetitive actions to supersede deliberate negotiations to the overwhelming detriment of the outcome.

Life, like golf, is a process of concentrated effort and nothing less will result in the superior adventures we are seeking. Think with me. . . . Consider that last muffed shot due to hurried preparation or a nonchalant attitude that you simply can't miss compared to that last costly business decision that wasn't given proper consideration or evaluation. Happens!

On 17, that "lurking danger" is a meandering little creek too wide to jump across and too deep to wade that lends itself to gobbling up any shot that gets away from you to the right. If you go over that little stretch of water, you may as well be O.B. 'cause you can't get to it anyway. Not so far right and you are wet. However you piece this one together, you have just cost yourself a stroke simply by failing to concentrate on the left side of the fairway. I mentioned a long time ago that there is a reason the well-manicured short grass between you and the green is called a *fairway*. More of those *fairways* hit have a tendency to calculate into lower scores at the end of the round. Name of the game, my friend.

By the way, I noticed a couple of guys a few holes back who had to be "eaten up" (slang term, I guess) with laziness or lousiness or possibly both. I will let you determine which one should receive the highest honor. Totally ignoring signs which a blind man could read with glaring instruction that no carts were allowed beyond that point, those two almost drove over one in pursuit of their destination. Excuse me -- I forgot. Some people are exempt from such menial things. Right? Laziness or lousiness?

To add insult to injury from my standpoint, those guys drove their cart up on the fringe of the green, hopping out to putt like they owned the place. Don't think they did. Laziness or lousiness? And to make

LIFE IN 18 HOLES

matters <u>even</u> worse, returning to the cart, they paid no attention that the fringe was wet and that the cart was parked uphill, and went spinning off to the next tee box leaving some really bad erosions for the greenskeeper to deal with. Laziness or lousiness?

Often I just have to shake my head at the inexcusable actions of inconsiderate people. I realize you don't see that too often on the golf course, but anytime is one time too many. But, hey, I solidly believe that type of activity is borne out of everyday developments of immature, self-centered, and belligerent members of the human species who consider themselves undauntingly superior to the rules of engagement that threaten their existence but only lend themselves to the conformity of others. I know. . . we will always have them. But arrogance and the sheer feeling of superiority completely get my goat! I don't know how you feel. That kind of action may have a place, but that is a place I need not be treading in. Cut me some slack – occasionally <u>you</u> need to vent, too!

Determined by your distance off the tee, you may have an 8 iron or a wedge left into a large green with considerable undulation. Three sizeable bunkers skirt the short grass to the left, but are not terribly threatening. Worth repeating. . . this is actually a very easy hole that yields some good scores.

Question? Do you not think we need occasional "easy" experiences as we negotiate this thing called *life*? I don't think there is any question about it. Should every task in life be a monumental undertaking we would find ourselves constantly "burning the candle from both ends" and before too long something would have to give. I heard Masters Champion Bubba Watson make a statement something like this: "If every hole on every golf course was a grind-it-out, exhaust-every-shot-making resource with no room whatsoever for error, at the end of the day we would all be looking for another occupation." There are probably certain personalities that can stand that kind of pressure. For most of us, however, majoring on the majors constantly is just not an option.

Minor strategies that push minor developments that result in

EASY PEASY

winning accomplishments are just plain ole necessary along the way. I'm sure that is why in the course of an entire PGA season, only four major tournaments are held. Even the best there is at playing this game of golf, the PGA professional, could not withstand the pressure of competing on that magnitude of a stage week in and week out. There has to be a little "easy peasy" scattered along our pathways of life. Up until now there have only been five *grand slam* (means they have won all the major championships) winners in professional golf. I doubt that changes a lot.

Pulling my Callaway Optiforce 460 from the bag, there is only one thought in mind. To me left center of the fairway is my only option and length off the tee is not absolutely critical. Reaching in two is not a problem, but water on the right certainly is. Have you heard the saying, "Keep it simple, Stupid"? Well, this tee shot is definitely a no-brainer. As the club head made contact with the Pro V, I really had no reason to look where my ball was going. You know what I mean. The sound, the feel – there was no doubt about the result. Of course, you can't keep from looking and as I watched my ball hit and run right to the middle of the fairway some 130 yards out, I started concentrating on my next shot. Preparation time is never wasted time and the ride down the cart path was satisfying to say the least.

Pin placement is back middle today and a good, smooth 9 iron is perfect for this approach. Standing behind the ball and visualizing the shot, I can't help but recall the first time I played this hole with my wife Kerry riding the cart with me. She doesn't play the game but enthusiastically breathes in the atmosphere and scenery on this course. Pretty much in the same location with 9 iron in hand, I hit behind the ball and came up short of the green. This beautiful piece of human flesh who is my greatest admirer, greatest influencer, greatest promoter and supporter, **and** greatest critic, nonchalantly looked at me and announced, "THAT'S PITIFUL!" Of course she was right, but at that particular moment I didn't need honesty. Sympathy would have been much more soothing.

This time was different. Pin high but I pushed it a bit, leaving a fairly long putt over a little ridge that necessitates carrying or it will come right back to you. Determined not to leave it short, I rolled it some six feet by and walked off with a par. Still, I stand behind my evaluation of #17: "Easy peasy!"

Next opportunity you have, check out *The Greatest Game Ever Played*. Based on a true story, I think you will find it intriguing, captivating, hilarious, and even thought-provoking. Harry Vardin was a gentleman as well as a professional. Francis Ouimet never turned pro, but won several prestigious tournaments as an amateur. Little Eddie will grab your heart and keep it if you are not careful.

Come on! Let's see what 18 has in store.

CHAPTER **18**

BRINGIN' IT TO THE CLUBHOUSE

WHEN PAYNE STEWART won the U.S. Open in 1999, one of the most riveting and lasting moments of USGA history was captured on film. This special moment has been played countless times and no doubt will continue its long-running saga. After Stewart made his final putt to win, he embraced young Phil Mickelson, looking him directly in the eye and urging him to play on and never give up. Phil finished second on that day, but has since gone on to become a major champion himself only one win away (the U.S. Open) from completing the grand slam. Payne established himself as one of the greatest ambassadors the game has known. His life cut short as the result of a plane crash, this icon of the game was not only a tremendous champion, but he also embodied the true personage of a husband and father.

Settling into the cart for the uphill ride from #17 to #18, I relish the fact that I am not walking this course and carrying my clubs. That, however, is not my main thought. Like Stewart and Mickelson (who is also a hero for the family), I think of how privileged and blessed I am to spend my days with a beautiful and wonderful Christian wife. Our children are both special and unique in differing ways and have filled my life with enormous excitement as I have watched them grow, mature, and prosper. Not to mention my daughter's three little boys who think Pap is the greatest.

Never. . . never. . .never underestimate the power and influence of a Christ-centered family. Hold on with a claw-like grip to those you have been given, never taking them for granted nor failing to show and to tell them how much you love them. We have no assurance of tomorrow, but we can create lasting and riveting moments today.

A great baseball legend, Joe Nuxhall, player-turned-announcer, was known for this great lament: "Rounding third and heading for home." That is kinda' the way I feel as I top the hill and catch full view of the clubhouse that sits directly behind and above #18 green. The landscape is gorgeous and the sense of once again completing another round and bringin' it home is enormous. Even though this is just a game, there is something rather special about knowing you are finishing.

My son and I often talk about "finishing strong." I have to ask. . . . How important is that to you? And you know, it really doesn't matter <u>what</u> we are finishing. For my son it was completing his Mechanical Engineering degree and later his MBA and finishing up with a *bang* instead of a *blister*. For you it may be just playing #18 with total concentration and logging the best score you have ever had. Or it could be completing a project, earning a promotion, or simply spraying some Armor All on your tires after washing the car. Gotta' have the tires looking good! It's kinda' like putting on scuffed-up shoes with a nice suit – there is just something drastically wrong with that.

So . . . what is it for you? Only YOU can determine that and only YOU can put the emphasis on "finishing strong."

For me there have been some excellent finishes and there have also been some weaker moments. But think about it. Sometimes those not-so- good finishes may be the catalyst for something even more important to come **if** we have learned from our weak performances. There is, however, one final strong finish that I am even now in training for and looking forward to. You see, my greatest life goal is to be successful at spending eternity with my heavenly Father after this brief stint of leaving my mark on society is over. Talk about a hole-in-one!

So I can never quit training, never quit equipping, and never quit

BRINGIN' IT TO THE CLUBHOUSE

anticipating when that strong finish is going to take place. I have to be ready and everything happening in this thing called *life* is forging me for exactly that. I emphasize. . ."strong finish."

Gliding to a smooth stop alongside the tee box, I am amazed at how pristine and beautiful the topography is in front of me. I am just going to sit here for a moment and soak it all up. Ever had one of those moments where you didn't want to go on to the next thing because you wanted what was "in the moment" to last? I know the "right now" is probably not going to affect how I negotiate through the rest of my life, but it surely is a pleasure to be in it. Perhaps I should try to describe for you what I am seeing.

To my left at a distance, I can see #10 fairway and green. Poplar and pine trees do a perfect job of separating the two fairways, still leaving ample opportunity to play from the wrong short grass if you have an errant shot from either tee box. Immediately in front of you is a links-type setting with a sage-looking grass growing rather tall. White and red tee boxes are out there too. Just beyond the tall grass is one of the most beautifully architecturally designed fairways you can imagine. A short expanse of flat ground gives way to rolling topography that will quickly cause you trouble to the right if you find the right side of the fairway. From there a deep swale leads to another totally flat piece of ground that, at its farthest point, provides an easy approach to the green. I don't think I mentioned – this is a long par 5. There can be some trouble to the right along this stretch, but not bad unless you completely stink it up. From there on in it is uphill to a large green with a lot of movement in several different directions. Funny, but it seems the pin-placement guy has a tendency to leave his mark on our futility by constantly digging his next hole right on the break of a slope. Oh, well, such is LIFE! Standing on the green and looking back toward the box, I almost believe the adorning beauty of this hole is even personified.

Did I mention this is a long par 5? I know this can be a bewildering game and one that plays with your psyche. And one of those seemingly hypnotic thoughts that seems to capture our intellect is that we have to hit the ball a **L-O-N-G** way. But allow me to intervene with this thought. A well-positioned tee shot, for instance, may prove much more beneficial to final score than a lot of yards off the tee that leaves a less than desirable second shot. Don't get me wrong. I would love to hit it a long way and leave it exactly where I want it. With that combo, you could turn pro.

Using the tee shot off 18, let me give definition to what I am talking about. A well-placed high on the left fairway tee shot landing 220 yards out can find its final resting place perfectly positioned 275 yards from you with an absolutely flat lie. The other scenario could be a 300-yard drive that catches the swale, funneling right completely off the short grass and leaving a very difficult second. So . . . do you have to be LONG OFF THE TEE?

Allow me, if you will, to give even more clarification to the point I am trying to make. Perhaps I am doing this because I am getting old and can't hit it as far as I once could. But anyway. . . we generally envision the touring pro hitting the ball a ton and always taking advantage of all that length. Well, take in this little morsel and taste it. When Hosea Maria Olazabal won the Masters -- I believe it was in 2009 -- he averaged 239 yards off the tee. You got it right! 239 yards. Heck, I can hit it that far! But what this tells us is that he really did an excellent job of course management, hit some tremendous iron shots into the green, and his putting was out of sight. You tell me. . . . Do we have to be long off the tee? There happens to be a lot of other aspects of this game that are critical to going low.

This green is just not reachable in two for me. However, when teeing it up, I concentrate on using all the left side of the fairway I can in order to take advantage of optimum roll. Pulling off the near-perfect shot leaves me an excellent flat lie, a 3 metal second shot, and then a good full sand wedge that at the least will find middle of the green.

To make a long story short, I just pulled off those two first shots to perfection. Actually, the Pro V came off the driver like a laser. Distance was a little better than usual and watching my ball roll out

BRINGIN' IT TO THE CLUBHOUSE

was incredible. That little round, dimpled object of manufacturing excellence came to rest at the extreme far end of my intended landing area. I could not have hit my 3 metal any better. Low trajectory and as the old saying goes, "straight as a stick," the ball came to rest on the up slope dead at the pin that was located back right. Driving up the cart path, I realized sand wedge was too much club.

Cart markers, "No carts beyond this point," were well out in front of my ball. Coming to a stop on the concrete path, there was no need to walk down to my ball to shoot the distance. With little thought, I pulled the lob wedge and quickly covered the distance. Talk about an adrenalin rush! I was pumped as I stood behind the ball lining up the shot. The ball came off the club face with a lot of height, and plopped down some twelve feet from the pin and never moved. Could have been closer, but I will take it. Back to the cart and a short drive on up the path, I pulled my Odyssey White Hot #2 with the 5.0 Super Stroke grip.

Pulling the flagstick, the thought just hit me. I am putting for another birdie. Make this putt and it's a five-under round of 67. In all honesty, I have never shot a round like this. I have already exceeded my best round ever on Old Silo, and making this putt would be icing on the cake. Sizing up this putt, the line looks like a major highway right in the middle of the cup. "Keep the head still, shoulders square, and let the arms swing freely" is what the putting gurus say to do. "Ten-four!" Man – I pushed it and came up exactly hole-high, dangling on the right lip of the cup. Waiting... waiting.... It is **not** going to drop. Tapping it in, I thought, "Almost." But still a good par.

Too much pressure of the self-imposed nature. You know what I am talking about because sure, you've been there. Why do we do that? It is not as though there is not enough of all kinds of other stuff going on in this thing called *life*. It really isn't necessary that we add anything to it. Remember that the next time you are standing over your next obstacle.

Four under 68. What a day! I am blessed!

CONCLUSION

WHAT MATTERS NOW?

"SCHOOL! I DON'T need it and I'm too busy." Totally out of the blue, my 3-year-old grandson made that statement to his mother. I don't know if it had anything to do with his mother's homeschooling her other two older boys, but needless to say, it really created a hysterical response from all of us. I've since wondered: What was going on in that 3-year-old mind that resulted in the regurgitation of that volley of words? Really kind of profound!

I have also wondered. . . after finishing up 18 holes of life, what are people really experiencing from a malaise of thoughts and decisions that are oozing from the craniums of human perception? I have come to the conclusion that a large majority of people simply don't care, have no clue as to where they are taking life -- certainly in this case, life is simply dragging them somewhere -- have no ambitions to fulfill, and have relinquished themselves to an entitlement mentality that will lead to a bogus outcome. "NEWS FLASH!" That ain't true for many! Where do _you_ fit in the equation?

Do me a favor. Think about when you took your test for a driver's license, and then simply keep pushing that thought out further and further. I lived in the country near the county seat which was a relatively small town. I took my driver's test there and became very familiar with the course I would be driving because everyone always went the same way. I also knew who would be giving the test plus I knew a lot about his interests. Let me interject something here. To be successful at anything, you need a plan. My dad owned a 1950 Ford pickup (Oh, to have it now!) and that, my friend, is what I drove for my test. I prepared, I practiced, but I also took with me the very latest (just released) copy of *Field & Stream* magazine and laid it on the front seat. Seem strange? Well, the person giving me the test was an avid **hunter**. When we got in the truck (Did I mention it was deer season?), he picked up that magazine, his eyes lit up, and off we went. I did NOT drive the same course as everyone else. I don't even think I parallel parked! And that was one of the greatest drives of my life. Passed with flying colors! Did I cheat? Not me! I merely had a well-thought-out, workable plan.

Let's keep pushing this thought. When I got my license, I just wanted to drive. Anywhere. . . everywhere. But as I grew older, the excitement of just driving kind of waned and destination became much more important. Now I seldom drive just to be driving. I know where I need to go and I go. However, that doesn't mean some of that need is **not** the destination of pleasure. Nonetheless, I have a needful destination. Let me ask: Do <u>you</u> really care where you are going? Do you have a clue? Are your ambitions driving you in the right direction? Or are your frustrations hindering what could be excellent results? To become successful at something -- at anything -- you must make a decision to commit to EXCELLENCE. Take responsibility. Be action-oriented! I remind myself of what my 3-year-old grandson said. "Don't need it. Too busy." Are you "too busy" to sit down and put together a detailed plan? Are you working on the most important things -- or are you just working? BUSY?

Professional athletes always have a well-thought-out plan prior to the beginning of any game. They have a visual picture of the outcome. They are so focused! Well, if you have read all this stuff, I'm quite sure you have seen nothing in the 18 holes of golf that was professional. But please bear in mind, it was only an analogy. But if you have thought anything about LIFE, the result must be one of different perception. Just like the pro athlete, there must be laser focus on the outcome. You must have a well-conceived visual plan. Not just a plan, but an in-depth, analyzed plan. And once this plan is in place, you have to work it every day. Good plans get tweaked. Good plans even change dramatically. I have read that great companies always have a great business plan at their inception. But I have also learned that great company success stories seldom mirror the original plan that ushered them into existence. Don't be afraid to whittle away at that stick you first put the knife to.

I mentioned that I considered my grandson's illustration to be profound. *Profound* meaning: having or showing great knowledge or insight. Well, maybe not! But let me ask, "What really matters now?" After you walk off #18 green of LIFE, perhaps you should sit down and do a recap of what you have just accomplished. For many this will mean a visualization and for others it will truly be a replay. How did you fare? Have you learned anything? How will you apply those things? Any deep reflection or insight that may indicate doing things differently is necessary? OR perhaps you just made a 40-foot putt with three different breaks downhill all the way and the speed had to be perfect. I suggest you put that one on mental deposit and write a check on it when the need arises at a later date.

You know what? Golf is a great game. It is fun, it is challenging, and it doesn't matter **who** -- everyone can play. Think. . . . The game is played in competition with the course and every course plays to PAR. Regardless of the score you shoot, remember: Keep your life in the FAIRWAY. Do me a favor. Go read Proverbs 3:5,6. Follow the advice and there will be some birdies in your life. Or who knows? Maybe even a HOLE-IN-ONE!

IT MATTERS!